T0198635

OTHER TITLES BY THIS AUTHOR:

And Rainedrops Fall Down My Cheeks (2010)
And Rainedrops Fall Down My Cheeks (2014) 2nd Edition (2014)
And Rainedrops Fall Down My Cheeks **Book One** 3rd Edition (2015)
Rainedrops From Heaven (2014)
Rainedrops From Heaven **Book Two** 2nd Edition (2015)
Rainedrops Journey to India **Book Three** (2015)

RAINEDROPS JOURNEY
TO
INDIA

Book Three

Raine

BALBOA.
PRESS

A DIVISION OF HAY HOUSE

Balboa Press books may be ordered through booksellers or by contacting:

Balboa Press
A Division of Hay House
1663 Liberty Drive
Bloomington, IN 47403
www.balboapress.com
1 (877) 407-4847

Print information available on the last page.

ISBN: 978-1-5043-3445-7 (sc)
ISBN: 978-1-5043-3446-4 (e)

Library of Congress Control Number: 2016902909

Balboa Press rev. date: 03/07/2016

Acknowledgement

I am very excited to announce that this third book in the "Rainedrops" series is to be published by Balboa Press, a Division of Hay House.

It is such an honor to be published by such a prestigious publishing company and I would like to extend my thanks to Balboa Press for their support and encouragement.

I sincerely want to say 'Thankyou' to my agent in Balboa Press – Derrick Lopez. Derrick has been my rock opening up doorways both physically and within my being. Thank you Derrick, you are my champion!

*Life gives us
brief moments with another
but sometimes
in those brief moments
we get the memories
that last a lifetime*

anonymous

Dedication

To those souls whose journey in this lifetime is to toil the soul –
you are very loved and not alone . . . . . .

Raine

Contents

CHAPTER ONE

LIFE IS A JOURNEY

A bad fall and some small strokes, they had all taken their toll and Raema's frail, elderly body no longer served her very well.

Her mind was still sharp, this was what made life so difficult for her: she remembered everything but her body would not co-operate by allowing her the movement she had been used to having. This was one of those nightmares we all hope will never happen to us, but for Raema it was reality and that reality was cruel, it took away her independence and her only way of retaining some dignity was to refuse to take her medicine which was keeping her alive, so that maybe, just maybe, her frail body might be kind to her and allow her to move on to her next journey in life, wherever that may be.

So when it was time for Raema to have her medicine she was always difficult, fussy. She would say "No take it away I do not want it!" Then there would be the usual battle of wills between Raema and her family.

I came to meet Raema when I worked with her son, and I was a little unsure how she would receive me. Raema came from India as a young woman with her husband and small children; she had one more child who was born in New Zealand. I had been told her English was very poor. When I went in to meet this old lady I had no idea of the journey that she would take me on and the deep, abiding love that would develop between us.

But this was day one, and day one I was somewhat nervous and not sure of how Raema would feel about me and how I would feel about her.

It was a bright, sunny day when I entered the lounge where her bed had been set up so that she could be part of the family activities and see the comings and goings of those that lived there. The public nurse would come twice a week to shower Raema while someone in her family changed her sheets and freshened up her bed for her. There were other times when she didn't quite make it to her commode and needed her bedding changed and a clean nightgown.

It was so lovely to enter and not have the telltale odour of urine, everything smelled fresh, clean and cared for.

At first Raema refused to speak to me, but that was okay, I was introduced as a work friend of one of her sons, so she was unsure of where I fitted into the picture and was trying to suss it all out.

I look back now and know we were both trying to suss one another out. I decided to treat Raema as I would any of my other of my patients and talked to her naturally, just assumed she understood all that I said to her. I told her where I worked, that I was an Osteopath, and that I hoped she would be happy for me to call in now and then and visit with her. To each of these pieces of information I received a brick wall in response.

It became time for Raema to have her medicine and no, she absolutely refused to take her syrup and her tablets, there was no way there was going to be a meeting of goals; she was adamant that this was going to be a non-event!

I still do not know what made me do it beyond that my heart went out to this old lady. I felt so sorry for her situation and couldn't bear to see the sadness that was written all over her face. I stood up, walked to the side of her bed and took her hand in mine and asked her to look at me. Raema looked at her small hand in mine. Then she looked up at my eyes and she saw me smiling at her.

"Raema," I said, "it is time for your medicine and I would be so pleased if you would take it for me."

I kept holding her hand and, with my other hand I reached out for the spoon to be filled with the syrup. I then gently brought it down to Raema's lips and to everyone's surprise, including mine, Raema gently received the spoon like a little child. I remember smiling at her and telling her, telling Raema what a wonderful woman she was to take her medicine for me.

Raema took her tablets from me in the same fashion and her family where absolutely blown away – it had been so long since she had taken her medicine without any fuss that they were in a state of shock. I remember how funny I thought it all was, because Raema was like a little lamb for me and I didn't understand what all the fuss was about.

Before long the family would try to have me there as often as possible for medicine time. I treated my visits to Raema as totally normal; I would sit and talk to her and then ask her to take her medicine for me. She always did and it was the beginning of a special relationship that developed between us.

It was a very long time before Raema would speak to me, when she did it was in English. I remember the shocked I had at how wonderful her English was and wondered why her family had inferred she spoke little English! We had lots of lovely conversations about so many things and our friendship grew deeper as I was drawn to this wonderful old soul.

Perhaps my treating her as normal rather than as an invalid made the difference. My young daughter would enjoy sitting by the old lady's bed and chattered away to her, I could see the pleasure that this brought Raema, it was almost as if she had a new lease on life; she seemed so much happier.

I noticed that Raema liked to sit and hold my hand for as long as she could, and I became aware of the most bizarre thoughts when I would leave and head home. I would think to myself, *I hope I do not die yet; I have to be here for my daughter.* Then I would realize what I was thinking and tell myself not to be so stupid; what silly thoughts to have! But the thoughts continued their intrusion after every visit I had with Raema, and I became increasingly aware of how strange they were.

Meanwhile I could not brush my absolute tiredness aside, and I began to connect it to my visits to Raema. I started to experiment: if I made excuses and did not hold Raema's hand, I left feeling much more alive and did not have the bizarre thoughts about dying.

I also took notice of the times I would hold Raema's hands and really spend time with her. Always the tiredness was there after those visits, as were the crazy thoughts.

I knew my experience was directly connected to Raema – she was the key. She was like a child being able to tap into someone else's energy, which made her feel better. It was a bit like being given a lollipop and not knowing when to stop sucking on it. In fact, that was what she was doing: she was sucking on my energy and leaving me depleted afterward.

I felt such sadness, as I knew I had to cut down my visits to Raema; I had my own little girl to care for and had to be careful and responsible to my own needs. I had worked hard at putting up mental blocks, using visualisation to try to stop what was happening between us, but it was all for nought. I tried using Christ's white light to protect me. I tried every single thing that had worked in the past. Still, I could not block Raema's energies. I knew I had to stop visiting her, and I felt so sad for both of us. I knew the family would not understand why I had to step out of the picture. I knew I was about to cause some very deep hurts.

I felt mean, and it hurt each time I had reasons why I could not go when the family would telephone for me to visit their mother. I knew they were hurting and did not understand. I did speak to her son of hers with whom I worked in the health field, and he had an understanding of what I was experiencing. His understanding still didn't help make me feel any better, and I knew Raema had to be feeling let down and deserted.

It eventually got to the stage where the family would ring me at work when I was busy with other patients and beg me go to see Raema, as she was asking for me and would not take her medication. "She needs you," they would say and I cannot begin to express what a heel I felt and how mean I knew I must have seemed to Raema and her family. It was not easy to say no.

Raema's son, would explain that she didn't mean to take so much from me; she just knew she was feeling better and didn't know when to stop sucking. Well, "sucking" was indeed the key word! He hoped I would still visit his mother, he was caught in a difficult situation because he also understood why I had to stop going.

Eventually Raema suffered a severe stroke and had to be hospitalised. I went with her son to visit Raema in hospital, promising myself I would not touch her. Raema looked like a small child in that big hospital bed. She had lost so much weight, she looked frightened, vulnerable; my heart went out to her.

When the nurses came in, Raema blew me away as she introduced my daughter to the nurses as her granddaughter! I found it harder and harder not to physically touch Raema. But I couldn't do it, I so needed to comfort Raema, as we took our leave I reached out for just a short while to hold her and let her know she was loved.

It was just a short drive home, as we neared my home I began to feel weaker and weaker. Trying to get out of the car, I collapsed, I simply did not have the energy to get myself inside. I needed to get into bed and get warm very quickly. I thought to myself *this is ridiculous, what on earth is wrong with me I only touched Raema for such a short time.*

In the wee small hours of the night I was woken up with this tremendous pain in my chest! It was horrific, I could hardly breathe. The pain seemed to keep getting worse. I was simply beside myself with what to do to stop the pain.

Finally it subsided and I could breathe! The pain was vastly reduced and I could move around; slowly, but at least I felt in control of my body again. It had been a terrifying experience.

I took note of the time, getting in touch with Raema's son the next day. Sure enough, Raema had suffered a heart attack at the same time I experienced such horrific chest pains and the staff were amazed at how well Raema was doing that morning.

Wow. Well, well, well. I wasn't amazed! If I understood anything now, it was to understand I could not go near Raema again no matter how difficult the situation became. I could not go through that again.

I understood what I had gone through in the middle of that night and I understood how much it had cost me. Raema had not set out to deliberately hurt me. She simply knew she felt better when I was there, and using my energy she had been able to bring herself back to a stable position again.

This dear old lady whom I had grown to love so much, we seemed to have so much in common – I would never see her again. It just didn't seem fair. The way our energy interacted between us, prevented me from being safe around Raema. It was great for Raema, she was safe – it was me who suffered and took the brunt of it and I could not allow it to ever happen again. I had a daughter to bring up and be there for her, and she had to come first. I would learn to live with the condemnation from the family and the guilt that I felt.

CHAPTER TWO

OTHER MEANS OF COMMUNICATION

If I thought that my interaction with Raema was over, I was very wrong! I was in for a huge lesson of how our energy can be manipulated and how we can learn to protect ourselves.

I would be busy just working away and suddenly I would feel Raema's energy reaching out for me. Raema's need for me was so great, that whatever teachings she had received growing up in India, she was very advanced at sending her energy out to another and drawing them in.

It was a challenging time for me to learn quickly how to protect myself using Christ's golden light to keep me safe; yet also allow me to have the awareness of what was happening around me. I look back at that time of learning, I have so much to thank Raema for. She was a wonderful teacher, my hope is that I became the student she knew I could become.

I would feel Raema sending her love to me, I learned how to send my love back in return. I knew that she understood my physical absence, and that did not stop our spiritual understanding of one another, and Raema's teachings of communication.

I would say to Raema's son "Your mother says the roses have just blossomed!" Now we both knew that Raema was physically limited to the lounge in her home and not nearby the roses yet when he went to visit his mother, sure enough, the roses that she loved so much had indeed blossomed that day.

It was a time of learning, for me, for Raema and for her son. This son was born in New Zealand so he knew very little about India. He had not been taught about his parent's country. It would be an amazing journey for us all as I learned to communicate spiritually with Raema.

When Raema was admitted to hospital, again she slipped into a coma. I was at peace with my decision not to go to the hospital to visit with her. What I did not know was that my learnings with Raema had not yet finished!

It was on the seventh day of Raema laying in a coma that I had my first vision from her. She showed me lots of scenes, people and places. I knew what I was seeing was India.

One event I related to Raema's son; there was a scene of a very young boy, standing in the dirt and crying. He was standing outside a sort of white-washed wall and somehow I knew this was part of his house. The little boy would have been around 18 months to 2 years old and he was wearing some sort of cloth around his lower torso.

I was totally taken by surprise when Raema's son burst into tears, he was so visibly shaken. He sobbed and sobbed. He was extremely sad for his mother and his tears just kept flowing. Shortly after, he brought a photograph of a young boy to show me.

"Yes, that's him, that's the little boy I saw in my vision," I said.

This child was Raema's firstborn. He had died when he was only a few years old, Raema's New Zealand born son – he had no idea that his mother had carried her grief so silently all these years. It totally shook him that his mother had not been able properly grieve for her baby. Her support group had been left behind in India. She had never gotten over the grief of loosing her firstborn child.

What an amazing woman Raema was; a young widowed mother with no means of support. Raema had to house and feed her children in a strange country where she had little understanding of the language. There were eight children altogether. It takes a special kind of woman to survive in this situation. She saw to it that all her children went to university and had a good education. In those days there was no government support, she had to scrape together every penny she could just to feed her children, let alone house and educate them.

I learned to have a great respect for this lady whom I had come to love so much.

CHAPTER THREE

THE FIRST FAREWELL

I continued to receive visions from Raema as she deteriorated in the hospital. There were so many places she showed me, and I knew these were scenes in India that were important to Raema.

I saw wondrous mountains, very high mountains and wonderful birds, large birds, like eagles only different, and I could see and hear one "cawing" as he flew from around a mountain and down over water that seemed to be in front of me.

I saw a beautiful forest and within there was a cavern – "This is the jewel I am keeping for you," Raema whispered into my spirit.

I saw a village inside a mountain – so to make sense of this let me explain. If you took a mountain and then cut a U shape out of the middle of it, then built a village within that U shape, you have a village inside a mountain!

I had no idea what any of these things meant at the time because I had no other reference. I just knew that Raema was working very hard to show me these places, that they were very important to her.

I knew the moment Raema's spirit left her body. She was afraid – she did not want to go alone. She had fear. It was so sad to know she passed from her body in fear.

The family would not allow my friend to bring his mother's body into his home. With friends, we went to the funeral directors and spent our time saying our goodbyes to Raema. It was actually really more loving, because we all made the effort to be in this inhospitable environment – yet there was so much love.

We sang songs to Raema for her last night. We told stories. We talked about her early days, some that were present had been neighbours and they had known Raema from her early days and could tell us stories about how hard she would be seen working, long hours at any work she could find.

This was Raema's last night to be physically upon our beautiful earth, we wanted it to be a happy and loving night for her. The dawn would come soon enough and Raema would see her last sunrise with her earthly eyes.

Her son suddenly looked at me at some stage throughout that night and said "We've just given mum a Maori farewell!"

I smiled at him as he understood the spiritual meaning of singing to his mother for her last night, being with her as she watched her last dawn. The tears flowed down his cheeks with gratitude for the love his mother was receiving.

That last night we all slept on the floor together. Raema was covered with only a sheet. However her head was not covered and we could gently touch her cheeks in love, sweep her hair back from her forehead and sometimes even give her a kiss.

I was in a very deep sleep and very slowly I came out of the sleep because I could hear the most heart wrenching wailing. My heart went out to whomever it was that had come to say their last goodbyes.

The wailing felt so physically close to me that I felt they must be very deep in their farewells. I tried to lay very still so as not to disturb them. Eventually my curiosity got the better of me; I had to see who loved Raema so much that they would wail with such heartfelt emotion. I slowly opened my eyes, as it felt as though the person was right there front of me. I thought I must be facing Raema's body.

It was such a shock to open my eyes and find I was almost touching the concrete wall in front of me – I obviously was not facing Raema's body! I gently and slowly turned so as not to interrupt whoever was grieving so deeply and it was such a shock to see no one was there!

There was no person standing beside Raema - and still I could hear the wailing. With understanding I looked at my watch, it was 6a.m. I looked out the window and the sun was just rising. It was dawn. Raema was saying farewell to her last sunrise in her physical body, and I had tears flowing down my cheeks as the wailing continued so deep and heart wrenching.

I woke up her son and asked him "Do they wail in India?"

"I don't know," he said.

Well that was a great help wasn't it, but I already had my answer. I knew they wailed in India. In the same way I understood Raema was giving me her farewells. I felt so privileged, so loved, so very deeply loved to be allowed to share such a poignant moment.

CHAPTER FOUR

I AM TO GO TO INDIA

T he family were indecisive of what they would do with Raema's ashes. I stayed very quiet. I did not have a vote. I was so heart broken. I simply buried myself within my grief. I had loved this dear lady deeply. There were many spiritual things she had taught me.

One day her son said to me that he thought his mother's ashes should be taken back to India. Then he blew me away asking me to take her home!

"Why me? She is your mother why would you ask me to go?" I asked in shock. It was the last thing I had expected.

His reasoning was that she wanted to return to India – that much was clear to him from the visions she kept giving me before her death. I was the one she chose to share those visions with, therefore, I was the one she wanted to take her home. I must say it was the last thing I had expected to be put in front of me. At the same time, I could not fault his reasoning. I knew he was right. Deep within me I knew that this is what Raema would have wanted, and I could also feel her presence assenting to this decision.

It all seemed to happen so quickly. The visit to the sales consultant for travel, getting a visa organised, arranging time off work. There suddenly seemed so much to do. It was also not the greatest timing for travel to India as there were regular publications in the newspapers about the uprisings in Punjab, India. There were clashes between different factions. There were so many terrorist reports. It was definitely not a safe time for a white woman to be travelling around Punjab alone.

However there is an old saying "ignorance is bliss" and I felt no fear of taking this trip. I felt very much protected and *I knew* that I would return home safely. It is also very true that if we knew what was around the corner in our lives, some of us would never take another step – but then think of the learning we would miss out on.

I had a long journey to make from New Delhi into Punjab, something like a 6 hour train ride so I decided I would take a domestic flight to reduce the travelling time. I was telling friends who were from that part of India about my upcoming trip and that I had booked a domestic flight from New Delhi to Armritsar. They were adamant that I should not take this flight – "Because they blow up the planes!"

"Well OK, I will take a train."

"No, no you must not travel on the train; they put logs across the railway tracks and rob everyone!"

"Well then I shall take a bus and I shall be safe," I replied.

"No. No, you must not travel by bus, they blow the buses up and you will be killed!"

Mmmm my options were becoming limited so I decided I would stay with the domestic flight I had booked and take my chances, after all it didn't seem which mode of travel I chose they all had their drawbacks.

Approximately a week before my departure for India I had a strange dream that is still with me today. I can relate it as though it were last night's dream. I dreamed that I was taking a domestic flight in India. I was on the way to the airport. I was only across the road from the airport. I was carrying my suitcase and in my other hand I was holding the hand of my young daughter. My daughter kept pulling me away from the airport and slowing me up. I felt like I was trying to move through an unseen barrier. It was like walking through thickened water. I was simply getting nowhere. I knew that if I did not hurry up I would miss the plane. I could see the airport which was a fairly dull design, made from concrete and just a square or oblong type of shape. I could see windows where you entered the building.

In my dream I am saying to my daughter to *please come on and hurry up or we will miss our flight.* Just then I saw our flight leave and my heart sank with disappointment. I watched the plane rise at quite a sharp angle in the air as it took off. The plane climbed quite high, I could see the fluctuations in the air as the heat seemed to be fired out of the back of the plane. Suddenly there was a loud explosion. I watched with horror as the plane blew apart in front of my eyes. I felt so shocked because I *knew* that had my daughter not delayed me, we would have been on that flight.

It was about that moment that I woke up with a deep knowing that there was no way in the world I was getting on the domestic flight I had booked. As soon as the travel office was open I was on the telephone cancelling that flight! I felt if ever I was to receive a message from Spirit – this was it and you could not have dragged me on to that plane.

I decided I would make my arrangements for travel from New Delhi to Jallandhar once I had arrived in India. It seemed the most sensible option.

Strangely, the first week upon my arrival in India, there was a domestic flight from New Delhi to Amritsar, the same route I had booked – it was blown up in the sky. I was so grateful to my angels for looking after me and keeping me safe! Was that the flight I had booked? I do not know, but it was enough to have had my dream affirmed. Here I am in New Delhi, at the same timing of my original booking, and there is a plane blown out of the sky! I could have been on that flight!

I had never travelled so far from my homeland before so this was quite a big thing for me to be doing. I have to admit to some excitement of what was ahead for me. I might not have been so excited had I known what was to greet me at the airport!

There were no arrangements for anyone to meet me at the airport. I would be arriving around 2 a.m. when the city would be sleeping. I was told by friends that it was quite normal to lay down on your suitcase, have a sleep then leave the airport at daybreak. They said that under no circumstances should I leave the airport until day break, marauders roamed and I would be found with a knife in my back and robbed. I figured I was most definitely staying on my bag at the airport until dawn.

What was not figured into the equation was that enroute to India, during my flight time, a military coupe was taking place and the Prime Minister had been fired upon. I believe he was shot but not killed. So it was with bewilderment when we arrived at New Delhi airport to be greeted by soldiers threatening passengers with AK47 rifles. The soldiers were waving them menacingly in our faces; in short, threatening and succeeding in frightening everybody.

I was expecting to see a busy airport once I was through customs, with shops open and people sleeping all over the place. Nothing! All the shops were locked down. There was not one soul sleeping on their suitcase on the floor. We were told very clearly that we were to follow the soldiers and leave the airport immediately. Oh great! I really needed this sort of welcome to India and I thought *what on earth have I gotten myself into.*

It was of interest to me that the airport looked just the same to me as it had in the dream where I had seen the plane blown up.

There was only one place open and that was a Change de Bureau which I needed to access as I had no local currency. I made my transaction with a soldier frowning at me and pointing his rifle at me. There was no way I was going to leave the airport and be left alone in the dark with nowhere to go so I was going to have to tough this one out.

I could see through the windows that there were people outside waiting to meet their loved ones from the flight, but there was no one to meet me. I could not go out there. As we were led in a line towards the external door I saw a small gateway that led to some seating that was fenced off just inside the windows and I thought that I could sit there and be safe until the morning. There was just one little problem, there was a soldier guarding this small gateway and he had a very scary looking rifle.

I stepped out of the line moving towards the external door and attempted to move through the little gate. Suddenly the soldier was screaming at me, pointing his rifle in a threatening manner right in my face and he was determined not to allow me entrance.

"Is there a problem? Is there a problem?" said an airport official rushing up to me.

"Yes, there is," I said to him. "I need to go and sit on those chairs until the sun comes up I cannot go outside now, I *need* to be able to stay inside the airport."

"Well you tell him," said the man indicating the soldier and throwing his arms up in the air. He walked off and left me! Well, that was a lot of help. I had to take this into my own hands and just deal with it. Oh boy, I was scared. I was so very scared.

I had never been in a situation like this before and certainly never had a rifle pointed at me, point blank in my face with someone screaming at me in a language I did not understand and so full of anger!

"I need to sit on those seats!" I tried to be forceful with what I needed to do – then pretending to be very brave I simply walked around him, walked through the gate and sat down very quickly at the first seat I came to.

Well, what an explosion from the soldier's mouth that seemed to cause. He was furious with me and aiming his rifle at my head, pointing to the external entrance whilst he was screaming his head off at me. I simply sat there and put my head down.

What else could I do? I felt my life was about to end!

I sat there asking Raema what on earth had she led me into? All I wanted to do at that moment was get on a plane and fly home. I did not want to be there. I was terrified. I was alone. I could not show any weakness. I had to be strong or at least pretend I was even if I felt like I was dying inside.

It was a terrible introduction to India!

CHAPTER FIVE

STICKS AND STONES

I t was a difficult night for me. The soldier stood over me dutifully pointing his rifle just in case I suddenly might bring out a knife or do something threatening. The soldier had to think I was such a stupid, foolish woman. His superiors can be very proud of him, he watched this foolish white woman all night, never leaving my side.

At least I had the option of resting my legs on the chair next to me. Whilst there was no way I was ever going to be able to sleep in that situation I did manage to get a little rest, well if you can call it that. Around 5 a.m. an army vehicle pulled up outside and troops climbed down from the back of the vehicle. It turned out they were having a change of shift so my guard gave an account of me to the new soldier who came to stand by me. At least he did not point his rifle at me. Another hour and the sun came up, it was really quite beautiful watching the haze start to lighten the sky and I deemed it a safe hour to finally leave the airport and take a taxi into the city. I had taken note of a noticeboard during my night sitting in the visitor's area in the airport. I checked it out on my way out of the external door taking note of a hotel name and asked the driver to take me there.

As we drove through the roads I noticed these very thin, sticklike figures rising from the ground. I looked closely at what was happening. To my utter sadness these were human beings. They had nothing. Not even the shelter of a rock to see them through the night. As the sun rose so did they – slowly and stiffly. Some showed interest in a motor vehicle going passed, others carried on their way not having the effort to take any notice. I was very saddened by their plight. I had never seen this level of poverty before and it really tore at my heart strings. I felt guilty because I was carrying several changes of clothing and all they had was what they stood in, nothing else. The men had a cloth tied around their abdominal area and the women had a raggedy sort of shirt that was long. Some had long pants on. I felt very sad and knew there was little I could do to change their situation.

I had a suitcase with me, also a hand held bag which I took every where with me. Inside the hand held bag were the ashes of Raema. I had promised I would keep her with me at all times. I also carried the documentation that allowed me to travel with the ashes of human remains. For some reason the undertaker had put her ashes into two containers, not overly large and tucked those into the most garish, mustard colored bag made of crushed velvet. At least by keeping her with me I had no fear of her being stolen from me, that would have been a terrible disaster but it was no burden to carry her with me, she was light to carry and I felt much happier having her with me than leaving her behind in the hotel room that I was shown to.

I was quite distressed that the hotel room I was given had no key, there was no way for me to lock the door and feel safe. I complained at the reception area but was told that this was their policy and that none of the rooms had keys. It was a safety factor if the room had to be evacuated in an emergency.

Well you can imagine how I felt about that, so before even thinking of getting changed for bed that evening I was thankful to have found a chair which I could prop against the door, sitting on its back legs only, thereby jamming it and stopping any possible intruders.

I was very tired by now but as much as I would have liked to have a rest, the city was coming to life and knowing I would not be very long in New Delhi I wanted to see the sights.

I have a habit wherever I go of carrying with me a packet of Wet Ones. For those that the name is unfamiliar with, it is a sealed container, inside there is a moist roll of disposal, moist cloths about the size of a face cloth. I cannot tell you how many times those Wet Ones *saved my bacon* as they say. I was so grateful to have them. It became quite hilarious in the end the way they came to be used and I never stopped thanking my angels for all the helpmates I had.

I had been instructed before leaving New Zealand that I must never lose my passport or my airline ticket as they were worth a lot of money on the black-market. It would take three months to apply and receive a new passport from the New Zealand Embassy.

The plan was to have them strapped to my body but that unravelled very quickly with the military presence. I was not allowed to enter or leave the hotel without presenting them. The same applied for any little shopping areas I wanted to enter;

I had to produce my passport and my airline ticket. So I had to carry them in my wallet, but at least I could tape most of my paper money to my body.

Quite often around the shopping areas or even in the more remote areas where I did not feel terribly safe with the soldiers, I found the Wet Ones I carried to be quite a life saver. I was always asked to not only open my bag but to empty it as well. Now this is where it would get rather strange because it did not just happen once or twice, it happened *every single time* I was stopped and searched. Try to imagine an average size shopping bag, black, that you are carrying – you have emptied out every single thing in the bag, except, Raema's ashes in their bright, mustard colored bag that looked like a bright beacon at the bottom of the black bag. Not once did the soldiers see her ashes! They would look in my bag, really have a good look but they never saw the ashes. The first time it happened I couldn't quite believe it and thought they were overlooking her ashes. But no, there were times when I thought they were going to turn my bag upside down they looked so closely inside – they never saw her. It was as if the angels had closed over a portal that would otherwise have shown her brightly colored bag and she really was invisible to the soldiers.

It is hard to believe isn't it, that they never saw her, but I can tell you I was searched so many times a day by very demanding soldiers, that I believed a miracle was unfolding in my little black bag.

Then I would realise I was not particularly safe and need to move on so I developed this little pantomime that was so incredibly simple it is hard to understand how it worked – and it worked every single time.

Let me tell you first, that India was undergoing a terrible heatwave. Temperatures were reaching 50 degrees Celsius and more – locals were actually dying from the heat. It was frightening. If the locals couldn't cope with the heat how on earth was I supposed to manage? In fact there were times when the heat was so bad, I could actually feel my blood start to bubble in my capillary veins around my mouth. That is how it actually felt like and I thought to myself, *this is not going to be a nice look on my face as I age.* Yes I actually thought about that, and as soon as I could drink water I would feel the blood vessels start to settle down, so drinking water became a priority.

Now I will tell you about my little pantomime with the soldiers in this terrible heat.

I would make a big thing of lifting my Wet Ones container, carefully take one out. I would sniff it, pat it on one cheek and make noises such as *ohhh, ahhhh* and then pat it on the other cheek. I would then hand it over to the soldiers. Well they are looking at this clothe, feeling it, smelling it, and most funny of all patting their cheeks with it and smiling! Then that soldier would hand it to the next soldier. Whilst the soldiers were busy examining my Wet One; I would quickly repack my bag and quietly scuttle off out of sight, with a huge sigh of relief. I gave thanks to those watching over me from the other side.

Sometimes I would be out in the countryside where there was nothing but a water pump and the soldiers who would give me a hard time and I cannot express how grateful I was for the foresight to pack plenty of Wet Ones; plus the blessing that Raema's ashes were invisible.

Imagine how terrible it would have been had they seen Raema's ashes and demanded I opened her containers up – it is simply unacceptable so to the powers that showered blessings over me, I am eternally grateful.

My first day was long. I had been on a very, very long flight, approximately 16 hours. I sat for hours in a chair at the inhospitable airport. I was experiencing an unprecedented heatwave that I have never experienced before; however there was so much to see and too much noise from the city to rest.

I kept the same driver with me throughout the day. He had a rickshaw. I was absolutely petrified the first time we approached a round-about intersection on the road. Cars, bicycles, rickshaws, buses, trucks, they all went for it from every direction and I was so sure I was going to die. I screamed! I screamed my head off as loud as I could but even I couldn't hear myself over the racket that all these vehicles made as they beeped horns, rang bells, it was mayhem, absolute mayhem. And every round-about intersection was the same. I was sure I aged 10 years that first day!

With gratitude I survived! How we survived those intersections I will never know and for those who have travelled to India you will understand what I am trying to describe and the absolute fear you experience travelling on such unpredictable roads.

I saw New Delhi's Parliament House, I saw many wonderful places during that day but the one that stands out in my mind the most is the pyramid! Yes there is a pyramid in New Delhi, I had never known India had pyramids but I was fortunate to see one with my own eyes. I was absolutely fascinated.

I purchased some simple clothing that were of the style they wear in India because my common sense could see how much cooler I would be wearing these styles than my own clothing. Of course at the time, I did not know, however I would learn later that the style I had chosen was the style of Punjab.

Before leaving home I had asked my friends from Punjab what gifts could I take with me to Raema's family and they said nothing, that what I would take from home would be of no use to them and if I wanted to give them gifts give them money.

I started to understand that advice a little just with the realisation of how unsuitable my own clothing was for the conditions I was experiencing.

There were many beggars lining the streets, some were maimed terribly and it was shocking to my senses to see how badly some of them were maimed. I watched with horror as little girls around 5-6 years of age would be holding a baby in the middle of the chaotic roads begging for money and I would be watching holding my breath as the baby's head would be wobbling on its side and I would be terrified they would be run over, yet they always seemed to know how to survive. And the baby's heads were never clipped by any vehicle. Simply amazing!

It was becoming quite an education and this was only my first day!

I watched with wonder as a cow would wander into the streets and everyone would make room for this cow. No one ever tried to shoo it away! I had known that cows were considered sacred in India but I had not realised how far that sacredness went. The cow even entered a shop as I watched and the owner took no notice at all, it was all perfectly alright.

I had my first experience as I walked down the streets of coming across a sufferer of leprosy.

I had never seen this disease before let alone so close up. He thrust his disease eaten arm, or what was left it of it as he only had the first part of his arm to his elbow, into my face. It was so graphic. It was so horrifying. I was so shocked and felt such horror that to my shame I ran from him. I absolutely just took off and ran until I knew I was well away from him and safe. It was then I was able to think about my reaction to this poor individual and I was so ashamed of my actions. I vowed never to run from this disease again. I vowed that I could look at it close up and not be so shocked that I would run away.

There were many people with leprosy that presented themselves to me, begging, I never ran from them again. After my initial shock I was able to cope and not turn away in horror.

But it is a horrific disease and the sight of it deliberately shoved in front of your face is a terrible experience to have. I did not know it was so prolific in India and was not prepared for what had happened. I knew I could cope with other victims from then on and I did. It is not something I would wish on anyone.

As the day began to come to an end I had my driver bring me back to my hotel. We came back via the very impressive War Memorial and I had him stop there so I could pay my respects.

When we arrived back at the hotel he would not give me a figure of how much I should pay him. He left it up to me and said he would be happy with whatever I would give him. This was a difficult one for me, it was my first day and I had little understanding of what a man might earn in a day and what would be acceptable. I took out my wallet and gave him 500 Rupees which is not a lot of money in my currency at home so I felt it was a fair bargain. Little did I know, it was the worst thing I could have done. I had given him what would equate to about a years earnings for many of the people in his profession!

CHAPTER SIX

THE PALM READER

I entered the hotel very weary, hot, thirsty. It was so enticing when the Jeweller stepped outside his shop within the hotel and invited me in to just sit and have a nice cold drink of water. I thought to myself *oh here we go again another person trying to push a sale on me* but the need for a cool drink overcame any doubts that I had.

Jimmy was the Jewellers name and true to his word he brought a chair forward for me to sit on and he brought me a wonderful cool drink of water. Oh my, it tasted good and I obviously needed it very badly. Jimmy was very pleasant, he did not try to push his wares onto me to buy – instead he sat down on his side of the counter and just simply chatted.

Jimmy told me how he had many American friends and that they would return to the States and write to him. He said

I shall show you my greatest treasures; with that announcement he opened a drawer and brought out a small box that contained postcards. These were his greatest treasures.

"Go ahead, read this one to me," Jimmy asked of me.

I read the postcard and he asked me to read another which I did, and when he asked me to read more I realised he could not read them, he could not read English and the look of bliss on his face as I read to him chased away some of my tiredness and I knew it was a small thing to do for someone to bring them some happiness.

Suddenly Jimmy starts bowing and talking quietly in his language to the left upper corner of the room. He then does the same to the right upper corner of the room. I was aware of a change in the air and knew something special was happening around me but I did not know what it was.

Jimmy asked to hold my hand and as he looked at it he told me many things from my life that he could not possibly have known from just looking at my hand. He then told me that there were some who would stop me for whatever reason I was there and that I needed protection. With that Jimmy opens another drawer and lays on his Jewellery counter a large piece of black velvet and on it he placed some carved ivory pieces laying them out in a specific way.

"Pick one," Jimmy said to me, "I want you to choose one."

So holding my hand over the pieces of ivory I passed my hand over them trying to feel their energy and which one would call to me. It is a gift I have had, being able to feel the energy of objects and sometimes even gathering some of the history from it.

I felt drawn towards one particular piece. I chose it. I took it in my hand and I held it, looking up at Jimmy.

Jimmy looked back at me saying "There were originally thirteen now there are only six left, six more to come."

Reaching into his Jewellery Cabinet, Jimmy brought out the most beautiful crystal necklace. It was stunning. It was made of just about every crystal available in India, Carnelian, Amethyst, Rose, Jade, Moonstone and many more, each piece of perfectly carved round large beads of crystal separated by a small gold bead. It was so beautiful and he placed it around my neck. It was so long that it came down almost to my waist. I thought to myself *this must be worth a fortune,* I waited for the sales pitch to begin.

But it didn't.

Jimmy did not try to sell it to me. Instead he said, "I have one more thing for you," and reaching into another drawer he gave me a round piece of jade that had a small hole in the middle of it. It was a flat piece, absolutely smooth and polished. Again, this was no cheap piece of jewellery it was extremely well carved.

Jimmy then asked me to give him a 20 Rupee note. Jimmy then left his little shop, went to the reception, returning with the 20 Rupees in lots and lots of coins.

"This is for the children begging at the Temple," Jimmy said, adding "now it is time for you to go to bed and get some rest, tomorrow you need to go and buy your train ticket to go north."

I left Jimmy stunned. I was speechless. He had not asked for any money for this beautiful necklace I now wore, nor did he ask for money for the other pieces he had given me.

I had not told him where I was going or why I was in India. Yet he seemed to have it all mapped out in his brain and was interested in my wellbeing. I couldn't believe it. I also knew this was part of my journey and so I just accepted what had happened and did as he bid – I headed off to my room to get some much needed rest.

I made a phone call to New Zealand before going to bed, I called Raema's son to let him know how things were going and he was very concerned to hear about the experiences I was having with the military presence but most of all he was absolutely shocked when I told him about Jimmy and what he had given me.

"What! But they don't give you anything for free," he said stunned to hear about the gifts and the necklace that was now in my possession.

I was even more scared about not having a key to lock my room so when I showered I tried to fit all of my possessions into the bathroom – just in case! It was not a secure feeling.

The next day as I headed out of the hotel I was searched by the soldiers. Then guess who was waiting for me, yes – my driver from the day before. He knew he was on to a good thing and by now I had a better handle on what I should have given him the day before, but it was too late now so I went with the flow hoping I was safe in his hands.

I asked the driver to take me to the railway station to purchase a train ticket. It was not until we stopped I realised we were not at the railway station and I felt unsure of my surroundings. We were in a back road type of place and a man came out of a small office greeting me and asking me to please come in and let him help me. I felt uncomfortable in these surroundings as it was obviously not the railway station however I went into his office.

When we arrived my driver had quickly spoken to him in their own language, so I was not surprised when he announced he knew I was wanting to purchase a railway ticket. He announced that because I did not speak the language I would find it extremely difficult to purchase a railway ticket, but I was not to worry as he would make the purchase for me. I accepted his offer, it had made sense to me, so I agreed to allow him to do this on my behalf.

"I need your passport to purchase the train ticket for you," he said with a smile. Mmmmm, oooooo, this was a difficult one for me. Hand over my passport! Scary! I was in some back alley and this strange man wants to help me and now he wants my passport. *Oh what do I do?*

I was wearing one of my new 'local clothing' choices, and the necklace was around my neck but tucked inside the upper part of my clothing. I held onto the necklace and asked *'within'* what I should do, and I decided it was a safer option to let them have my passport than to put myself at any risk, so I handed over the passport and watched him walk out the door, hoping I had not made a poor decision.

It seemed forever waiting for the man to return, he must have been at least an hour and I was thinking surely it cannot take this long to purchase a railway ticket! Finally he turned up with my passport, my railway ticket – I paid the fee he asked for which was 800 Rupes. It was not until much later in my trip I realised he had been dishonest, but more of that later.

At least I now had my railway ticket and for that I was grateful, my passport was safely back in my hands and I had the driver take me back to the hotel, being sure not to give him as much as I had the day before, but what I felt was a fair deal.

I saw Jimmy at the Jewellery store and he asked if I had my railway ticket? I was able to confirm I had it and he seemed quite relieved for me. He said that had I asked him today to read my palm he would not be able to, it was not something he normally does. But every now and then he said, a special person would come along and it would come over him that he must do this service for this person. It was not something he had control over. I was quite shocked to hear that considering the gifts he gave me right down to thinking of the children begging and making sure I had enough change to give to them.

"I will see you when you return," said Jimmy.

CHAPTER SEVEN

A BUS IS BLOWN UP

I had time to kill after purchasing my train ticket so instead of heading straight back to my room I headed into what looked like a bazaar where there were many people of all colors looking and buying. I went through the same rigmarole that I had been going through with the soldiers to be able to enter the bazaar but it was totally worth it.

I saw some people that were extremely black, so much they were almost a blue/black color and they were so beautiful in very bright oranges, yellows and reds that they were wearing. They wore a different style to the local garments worn and they were absolutely stunning. I had never seen anyone that dark before but oh they had the most beautiful face contours and would have looked fabulous on any fashion catwalk! They were tall, slim but very voluptuous. I felt very dull next to them.

I was very thirsty and found a place I could sit and order a cold drink, mostly lemonade, fanta, coco cola, those types of drinks and I came across a young couple who were from, of all places, 'down under' – Australia. They were quite excited to meet someone from New Zealand!

I always call Australians our cousins across the ditch because we seem to be on our own at the bottom of the world when one looks at an atlas.

They were wonderful company and asked if I had met Sandy? Well no, of course I had not met Sandy but they were meeting up with her and she would love to meet me so we hung out together for a little while, before too long Sandy actually did come along!

Sandy was from the United Kingdom, she absolutely loved India, it drew her back every year so what she would do was go home for the summer period in the UK and work long, long hours saving every penny she could, then she would let her flat go and put her stuff in storage. Then Sandy would head off to India for six months of the year. This was her annual trek every year!

I was quite shocked when I learned she was only in her late twenties because she looked to me as though she was in her forties at least if not more and I thought that the climate and conditions in India had not been kind to her and by now it was showing on her face. I was sorry for her as she was so lovely. She recognised that she could live very well in India for very little money compared to living in the UK and I got a handle on what sort of money I should be giving the rickshaw drivers, etc. She was a huge help and I was most grateful.

They were all stunned when I told them how much I gave the rickshaw driver on the first day in India saying that was a years wages for him and please don't do that again because it is not fair to the others who are working just as hard and he will target me as an easy touch. So lesson learnt.

The day was growing later and everyone was ready to head off in their different directions so I deemed it a good idea to head back to the hotel. Guess who was waiting outside the bazaar for me to emerge? Yes it was the very same rickshaw driver and he most certainly had recognised I was an easy touch and was making sure no one else got a look in at taking me anywhere.

I still had to go through my little pantomime with the soldiers to be allowed to leave the bazaar but hey, it worked well so let's not knock it!

I felt as though I was in a cocoon and very much looked after by my angels and Raema. I had no fear whatsoever that harm would befall me. As my driver rode his rickshaw along the road we heard an explosion so horrific that it rocked the rickshaw and he stopped.

Literally across the road from us – terrorists had blown up a bus. They had set a bomb and blown the bus up and I saw the back of the bus fall away from the front of the bus – I truly did. I watched as people fell out of the bus, many of them obviously dead and those surviving were bleeding badly. There was such a lot of activity of people trying to lift victims out of the bus and lay them out on the walking areas to be attended to and I watched as they lay the dead out side by side on the road.

It seemed to go on forever that more people were emerging from this "crack" in the bus that left the back half completely gaping open like a huge mouth and there was blood everywhere.

Stunned, I said to my driver "The bus broke in half."

"Yes," he said, "it has been blown up."

"Okay we can go now I want to go back to the hotel." I was so protected in this cocoon that I was completely untouched emotionally by this horrific demonstration of terrorism. It went through my mind that friends in New Zealand had said to me that they blow up the buses and I must not take the bus to Jallandhar.

That realisation hit me, but the true level of horror that I had witnessed did not hit me until I reached the safety of my home in New Zealand. When it did hit me, oh it was so terrible. I shook and shook with horror and fright that they might follow me and I relived those moments from a totally different perspective. The cocoon had been lifted and I went into shock for about six months of all that I had been through.

I felt so inadequate and so guilty that I had a household full of furniture. I did not want my possessions, it seemed so wrong to have so much when I saw many with so little.

I knew what made me very rich.

I knew I was very rich because I had a tap in my home and I could turn it on and have clean drinking water that would not make me sick.

I also understood what else made me very, very rich.

I had a toilet in my house, and I could flush it after it had been used. Oh My God! I was so rich, how was it possible that I had so much and these people had nothing, I felt like I was an impostor on the earth and that I did not deserve to be here. I had guilt, guilt, guilt. It was coming out of my ears I felt so guilty. I wanted to give it all away.

It took a long time for common sense to prevail and for me to understand that this was what my life was like in New Zealand, and I had been given a glimpse of ordinary life in India. There are few words for me to describe the uncleanness of my wealth. It truly would have been around six months for me to come to terms with learning to live my life again in New Zealand on good terms with all that I had.

There really was no alternative.

I truly understood just how much I was protected when I had been on my journey to know that the terror of a bus being blown up directly opposite me had so little effect on me at the time.

What amazing blessings had protected me and kept me free of what would normally send me into a deep hole of depression and terror. I had so much to be thankful for to my angels and to Raema.

I cannot begin to express my gratitude!

CHAPTER EIGHT

JOURNEY TO PUNJAB

I was up early and at the train station with plenty of time to spare. I had no idea how busy the station would be and wanted to be sure I would not miss my train. It was a good thing I went early as it was absolutely crowded!

My usual driver indicated to a man who came over and picked up my suitcase and after checking my train ticket, he carried my suitcase on his head through the crowds and I figured all I had to do was to keep up with him as he was moving pretty fast and all would be well. Little did I know of the trials ahead of me!

It was just as well the young man took my suitcase and knew where he was going as the train was so long I would have had no idea how to find my seat! As it was he went directly to the correct train carriage and took me inside putting my suitcase on the seat which I had booked. I had no idea how much to pay him but knew this was a service he offered and how he fed his children so opening my black bag that I was carrying, I took out my wallet and gave him a couple of hundred rupees. I placed my wallet back in my black bag, closing the bag. I lifted the suitcase up to the bag carriers above my seat and when I looked down, to my absolute horror my black bag was open and my wallet gone! The thief was that fast. I had not seen nor heard anything out of place.

Oh nooooo, this can't be true I said to myself. I tried asking the people that were sitting within my carriage if they had seen who took my wallet but no one answered.

My passport and my airline ticket were in that wallet and I desperately needed it back but even I could see that I could do very little about it. I walked out to the door where one enters the carriage looking around and then holding onto my necklace (that was tucked inside my clothing for safety) said a little prayer and asked my angels to help me, I was in trouble and I badly needed some intervention. *Oh please help me!*

Upon returning to my seat, just a few seats behind me a man was sitting – he had not been there before. I asked him if he spoke English and could he be of any assistance to me. He had excellent English and I was so grateful to have someone to talk to. I told him what had happened and he said that it was quite a common occurrence and that they were very professional thieves who moved very fast and knew what they were doing. He said there was a policeman outside on the pavement and would I like to report the theft to him.

So following this man, making sure to bring my black bag, we went looking for this policeman who was not very far away. The man spoke to the policeman, on my behalf, in their own language and then the policeman just walked away, so that was a great help! I could not believe his disinterest and he did not even try to question me. *Well he is a great help* I thought to myself.

We returned to our seats and I sat down feeling very shattered that I had lost my passport. I knew the airline ticket could be replaced easily, there was very little money in the wallet as most of it was taped to my body, but my passport! It was going to take me three months to get a replacement and I just couldn't spend three months sitting around waiting for a replacement passport. I had my clinic to run, bills to pay and they would not get paid if I was not at home working!

I pestered and pestered my angels for help. I had no idea what else to do and kept holding the necklace through my clothing and begging the spirit world for help.

The man sitting behind me said to me I had a decision to make – was I going to get off the train and go into New Delhi and report my missing passport to get the paperwork started or was I going to stay on the train?

"You need to decide now," he said.

I understood why he was pointing out to me that I needed to make a decision as the train was about to leave.

I thought carefully about it, I was feeling the crystal necklace through my clothing and asked internally *what should I do?*

Suddenly I *knew* what I should do and I said to the man "I already have my train ticket so I shall stay on the train and make a complaint to the police in Jallandhar and start the paperwork from there."

He seemed pleased with my decision and suddenly you could feel the train starting up getting ready to pull out.

It seemed almost immediately after that decision that there was another occurrence.

Suddenly the man sitting behind me comes to me and tells me there is a policeman outside our carriage asking to speak with me and would I like him to come with me and see what the policeman wants.

"Oh yes please I would be so grateful for your assistance," I said as we moved through the carriage door onto the carriage platform. There were dozens and dozens of Indian people surrounding the policeman and when they saw me they all reached up trying to touch me. I didn't understand at first what was going on. It was then that the man who came to help me answered my inner questions and told me what was happening.

Apparently the policeman had found my wallet on the floor of another train carriage on a completely different train and inside my wallet was my passport and airline ticket but of course there was no money.

"This never happens," he said to me, "your passport is worth a lot of money on the black- market and this is unheard of – they all want to touch you for luck because truly, this is a miracle."

Wow! I was completely blown away. My wallet was not only returned but my passport and airline ticket also came back to me!

I was so grateful, immediately I thanked my angels quietly within and held my arms out so that as many as possible of all the arms reaching for me would be able to touch me as the train began to leave.

I was so grateful for this incredible blessing.

He was correct, it was a miracle, just as not getting shot at the airport was a miracle, and Jimmy giving me so many crystals to protect me was a miracle. I had one miracle after another unfold for me and still there was more to come!

I sat down in my seat on the train feeling stunned that my important documents had been returned to me.

It almost felt like a test – what would I do in that situation and depending on my TRUST the rest would follow.

I had my miracle, my angels and Raema were looking after me and I was full of gratitude.

As I sat there I was surprised as the man behind me came to me and said "you eat, you drink when the boy comes round with the food and drinks and I will pay for it."

I was so grateful for his kindness. I could hardly say to him "Oh don't worry I have plenty of money taped to my body." It was better to let everyone think all my money had been stolen.

News of my miracle travelled quickly through the train. Amazingly, many more strangers came to me and they all said the same thing to me "you eat, you drink, I will pay for it."

The generosity of these Indian people astounded me. I knew how little they all had yet when they had heard my money was stolen, they came to my assistance. I was just so incredibly grateful and humbled by the kindness shown to me from so many.

Again, I knew my angels and Raema were continuing to look out for my wellbeing – I was safe. I had a six hour train journey ahead of me and I would be fed and given drinks. What more could I ask for.

It really was a miracle that I had my passport and airline ticket returned to me. I knew that would not normally happen. It was extraordinary.

I was so happy as the train pulled out and when the young boys came around with bottles of drinks and sandwiches I would make sure to eat and drink; but not too much as I did not want to cost other people too much money. I think this was when I started to fall in love with the people of India. They gave from their hearts and in doing so showered blessings upon me. How could I not love them!

It was a long train ride, six hours – but my surprises were not yet over!

I watched the landscape as we travelled many hundreds of miles. I looked for some recognition of what Raema had shown me in her visions, but nothing, no mountains anywhere. The land we travelled through was dead flat, not even a rise. I was surprised at how many hundreds of acres remained uninhabited then suddenly there would be thousands of people huddled together living under little more than rags propped up on sticks and there would be one tap that they all seemed to share.

The poverty was heart-breaking, so much land uninhabited and then suddenly tent city in the middle of nowhere!

I assumed, perhaps wrongly, that they gathered where they were because they were surrounded by fields and fields of rice, wheat, hundreds of fields of grains growing and even sunflowers whose flowers were larger than the size of my head. They would have access to food! But I was wrong. Their level of poverty was abysmal.

As the train continued on its journey, I watched as a woman with babies in tow crawled along the ground behind a man carrying a bag of rice on his head. A few grains would fall out as he walked along and she would meticulously pick up each grain from the dirt, and you simply *knew* that this was how she would feed her children that day.

We passed many fields of just red dirt, red because of the heat, and now and then there would be a very wide river with bridges for people to cross. Eventually I realized I was seeing the Ganges River. But no one camped next to the river to use that water so perhaps it was too sacred to use for living purposes, I didn't know, I was just surmising.

Not long before my train stop, a man approached me with impeccable English. He handed me 2000 rupees. I looked at him in shock; I could not believe he was giving me so much money. He told me I would need it where I was going and that he knew my money had been stolen from me. He also told me that he would arrange for transport for me from the train station to my hotel and that he would pay for the transport for me. Oh my goodness, I was receiving so much care from these kind people how could I repay them?

The man would not hear of me repaying him in any way so I asked about his family and his wife was pregnant with their first child. I asked if I could have his address and would he allow me to send some clothes for the baby from my home land and he agreed. I very gratefully watched as he wrote down his details for me and I did follow up when I returned home and sent a large parcel of baby wear for their new born. It was a form of repayment he could accept from me, repaying his kindness, and I was so happy to do this for him and his wife.

As promised, the transport was waiting for me and delivered me to my hotel safely.

Another miracle had unfolded for me.

I thought to myself, if this was happening in my homeland how many people would put themselves out and assist in the way I had been assisted in India. Mmmm, sadly I decided not that many would have come forward.

I was truly grateful for the assistance given to me, for the money given to me and all the kindnesses that so many showered upon me on my journey. I had been well looked after and now I had much to look forward to.

I did so love the heart of these beautiful people that surrounded me!

Miracles do happen!

CHAPTER NINE

JALLANDHAR

As I arrived at the Hotel in Jallandhar I was struck at how isolated it seemed to be in what I would call an industrial area. Down one side of the fenced hotel was even a little caravan selling hotdogs to people passing by but directly next to them rolling in the mud were these huge big pigs! They were literally just rolling around making piggy honk, honk sounds now and then and were totally happy in their mud pit that they seemed to have helped to grow and spill over onto areas that customers had to walk through to purchase their hot dogs.

I must say I looked at this with some trepidation and decided that this was most definitely not for me! I was so grateful that the hotel I had chosen had a restaurant and I did not have to go out to find food. Mind you it was quite disconcerting, my first meal arrived and I found a dead fly in the middle of the rice!

I complained to the waiter who simply removed the dead fly with his fingers and then smiled at me as if it were an everyday occurrence, which I began to learn that it probably was and I was making a fuss over nothing!

It did not give me the courage to venture into that restaurant again, and I believe that it was from that food that I developed what is commonly known as "Delhi Belly."

Ohhhh, if you have ever been victim to "Delhi Belly" you have my sympathies. It is truly not nice and in the time I had there I must have lost about three stones! Later I looked back on that incident and decided that perhaps I was going through a purification period for what was yet ahead of me.

I was very happy to find that my room had a key and it actually locked! I must say it gave me a huge sense of safety that the hotel in New Delhi had not given me.

I looked out my window, I had a good view as I was on the second story, their highest level. I overlooked the main road as people entered that area of town or left it. It seemed very peaceful looking out and I was very tired from a long, long journey fraught with danger so I was glad to turn in early. The evenings in India when I was there seemed to be very light until it got quite late so I did not allow the lightness in the sky determine what time I should be going to bed. I listened instead, to my body, and it was far more in sync with how I felt than how the sky looked!

CHAPTER TEN

THE TAXI DRIVER

I look back at that period in my life and think how dumb could I be? Almost all the instructions that I had was written in Punjabi and do you think I could work out where on earth I was supposed to be taking this lady's ashes? Not a hope!

I was shocked and had not been told that in Punjab almost NO ONE seems to be able to speak English. Oh my God what a terrible reality that was! I had been told of only one contact I was to meet and he was a taxi driver and if I found my way to the main taxi office I would be able to ask for this man because he spoke good English and he would be able to assist me.

Well, greater words have been spoken, but on the whole they have had something to back them up and give them authenticity. Something that was badly lacking in this particular place and time!

So far the only person I had met who had a little bit of English was the person who checked me into the Hotel in Jalandhar, but he was a strange person, I did not trust him and he looked at me as though he was leering at me. I did not feel comfortable with him at all. However he had agreed that I could pay my account using my Diners Card. Something that he reneged on when it came time for me to check out, I felt sure he was filling his pockets with an over inflated account.

That first morning in Jallandhar I woke with great hopes of finding my way to the main taxi office and getting some help as I was completely at a loss to try to read some of my instructions, and therefore had no idea where it was that I was designated to take Raema's ashes. I could not believe I had not double checked my written instructions before leaving New Zealand and I really was left out there, swinging on a limb with no idea where to go!

I decided I would forego breakfast since I had been up most of the night with "Delhi Belly" and was really quite reluctant to move away from my bathroom. I had to be brave. I was on limited time and I needed to find the taxi driver who spoke good English. I looked out my window and was quite disconcerted to see that during the night a road block was set up and soldiers with AK47 rifles manned all the main roads in and out of Jalandhar.

It was also obvious that I would have trouble leaving the hotel unless I emptied my black carry bag of all its contents as I would be thoroughly searched. *Oh gosh* I thought to myself *I sure hope these soldiers like the Wet Ones I have brought with me.* Experience had taught me the wisdom of strapping most of my money to my body and the fashion of clothing that I was wearing was in fact indigenous to Punjab! It consisted of loose, long pants and a matching top with V neck and ¾ sleeves. I had not realised this fact when I had made my purchases in New Delhi. I could see the good sense in wearing such a cool style in such heat. Of course everything was made in cotton and they had different decorations around the neckline that gave them some individuality and some were actually very beautiful.

I made my way down the stairs, slowing down carefully as it registered with me that, the foyer of the hotel was totally full of soldiers; they were standing around talking and the thought went through my mind *I hope they have not taken up residence in the hotel!*

Sure enough, upon leaving the hotel I was asked to empty my bag of everything so that they could inspect what I was carrying. Thankfully, as had happened before when they looked inside my bag, they did not see that brightly colored, mustard bag that was like having neon signs inside my black bag!

I was blown away, the soldiers did not see Raema's ashes. Somehow, from whatever dimension Raema was in, she had cloaked her bags of ashes; it was obviously important that I got on with doing the job that I was sent to do. Without other references to rely on, I pulled out my trusty Wet Ones. Well you just won't believe this but – yes, they loved my Wet Ones. I quietly and quickly put away everything that was on the ground back into my black bag and literally scuttled away!

Fortunately for me there was a driver and a rickshaw nearby who was happy to take me in his rickshaw, once we established where we were going to go!

It took some doing trying to relate to the driver that I wanted to go to the Taxi Office. "Taxi?" he would say to me.

"No, no I want Taxi Office," I replied and it would take some going back and forth before we decided on Taxi Office.

Well at least I had hoped he had understood me and was taking me to the Taxi Office.

I was relieved when the soldiers on the road opened up their barricade and allowed us access to go further down the road. They had obviously seen me come out of the hotel and deemed that it was safe to allow me to go.

A huge bird swooped down in front of us, actually I had never seen such a big bird that up-close before – then it flew high into the sky and I remembered seeing a large bird like this out of my hotel window the night before.

I wondered what on earth it was but knew it was hopeless trying to engage the driver into conversation. It was difficult enough trying to get him to understand that I wanted to go to the main taxi office.

"Ah, taxi," he muttered in Pidgeon English and I just hoped we were going in the right direction.

I actually felt quite guilty using his services as the roads were not paved as our roads are but were simply dusty, stone and dirt roads; the sweat just dripped off him as the heat wave continued. Still he cycled on as if nothing was a problem and he had my respect.

We pulled along the side of a very busy road, it was outside a sort of shed made out of various parts of aluminium and put together with a door and a tiny window where a man sat in the window

"Taxi Office," my driver says with a smile and his hand out for his fare, and, with the thanks of the gentleman on the train who gave me money, I had an idea of what I should be paying these drivers.

So here I am now, standing on the side of a very busy and noisy road trying to make myself be known and telling them who I wish to speak to.

"No English, no English!" the man shouted at me.

Oh dear, I am in a fix so I did the only thing I could think of – huh amazing what you do when you are desperate! I held on to my black bag very tight and tried running from vehicle to vehicle yelling on the top of my lungs "ENGLISH, DO YOU SPEAK ENGLISH! ENGLISH, DO YOU SPEAK ENGLISH" I was waving my free arm and I must have looked a ridiculous sight. Fortunately I did not get run over or hit by a moving vehicle, how I don't know I can only say that my angels were looking after me as I ran around like a lunatic!

I must have spent half an hour running up and down that road and I must have looked like a woman half insane! I looked like a half crazed woman, and, oh my God would you stop for someone like that?

But do you know what? It worked! It actually worked!

Even all these years later when I think of it, I cannot believe it actually worked!

This tiny little car drove to the side of the road and called out to me "I speak some English." Actually the driver spoke beautiful English and I told him of my necessity to get hold of the man who was written about in my written instructions and please, please, please would he help me?

The man from the car spoke to the man in the tiny little window and it appeared that the driver had been in an accident (no surprises there) but was due back any day now so I was invited to return the next day.

Well that's the morning gone I might as well take some time to look around.

I had absolutely no idea how to walk back to the hotel and wanted to get to know Jallandhar a bit better. You know the saying – no time like the present - so I strolled quietly along the streets and came to another type of 'Bazaar.'

I had the routines with the militia pretty down pat now and it didn't take me long to get them so interested in my Wet Ones that I was completely forgotten about. I am sure that purpose in using them could not have been more further from the inventors mind!

The days passed by and still no taxi driver turning up for work. I was beginning to worry that he was never going to appear when a few strange things began to come to my notice.

Every evening upon retiring, and every morning upon rising I was in the habit of looking out of my bedroom window. On each occasion this mighty bird was swooping up and down and round and round my window and as silly as it sounds, I began to feel that the bird was keeping an eye on me; it felt lovely, in a strange country, to feel as if their very own birds just might watch over me.

I had mentioned before that I was in a hotel seemingly in the middle of an industrial area. Well one day, walking home from nearby shops I had this very bad feeling come over me.

I wanted to go and hide!

Stop it you're being silly I said to myself!

Oh Noooo Oh please No I cried out to myself! I gripped the crystal necklace hidden behind my clothing and begged my angels for help! There was nowhere to hide!

I was on a dirty, dusty road with no one in sight – absolutely no one that I could run to – I was totally alone and very afraid. The fear I felt was palpable.

As I walked slowly along this lonely road, a vehicle passed me by, slowing down. It was an open army type jeep with about eight men on the back and still room for more. They were singing, from the tone of their voice and the physical actions they were performing – it was pretty clear what they meant as they pointed at me and jeering at me and were indicating that their driver should stop so they could take a closer look. By now I was standing very still, holding onto my hidden necklace and begging for assistance from Raema and my angels.

If they take me with them I will never be seen again, never. No one will ever know what happened to me.

The soldiers got down off the back of the jeep, they were talking and laughing, looking at me. All of a sudden something happened, I am unable to describe what brought about the change – but they couldn't see me!

They really couldn't see me and after a short time of looking around, and looking like they were wondering why they had stopped, they got back on their jeep and their driver sped off!

Oh my God, I cannot begin to tell you the relief I felt. I had been so afraid, actually I was terrified and now I was feeling *so* safe! I still had not moved as I was processing the fact that they had not been able to see me or they would have dragged me on the back of that jeep and I would have never been seen again, and still the street was empty except for one single thing besides myself.

Gliding on the air currents above me was a huge bird, and this time I was sure it was the same bird who had been circling my apartment!

I don't know what is going on here but I am so very grateful! I thought to myself.

CHAPTER ELEVEN

THE BLIND MAN

Time was slipping by and finally I made contact with the taxi driver that I was given the name of. I cannot begin to tell you the depression I felt when I tried to speak with him. His English was so poor it was non-existent and I cannot imagine anyone thinking he could speak English and guide me on my journey!

I walked away feeling very disillusioned. I had spent nearly two weeks waiting for him and for what – nothing. He was of no help to me whatsoever. I had to come up with another plan as I only had one week left before my plane was to fly out to New Zealand and I needed to be on it.

By now I had walked so many streets in Jallandhar I was fairly familiar with the areas I needed to go.

It was quite strange some days, I would walk down a busy street and everyone would stop what they were doing and stare at me. It was quite disconcertaining. I began to think that these people had never seen a white woman before, especially one on their own. I knew that it was most unusual to see a white woman walking these streets alone but surely they had to have seen this before. I could not have been the first they had seen, but it happened nearly everywhere I went.

So I was quite a spectacle. Apparently!

One day it was most interesting, I needed to find a banking institution and when I did it was quite weird because there was this very long queue of people waiting for them to open so they could enter the bank. Opening time came and they all rushed in at once and I was left standing on the street thinking how strange they do things in this country.

I entered the bank – and everybody stopped what they were doing, even the tellers. They stopped in the middle of counting money out for their customers! The whole banking area came to a standstill to watch me walk into the bank. It truly felt weird! I felt as if I was on show! You could have heard a pin drop.

I had no idea where to go as there were signs that I could not understand but I assumed gave instructions of what type of assistance was available at which counter. Surprisingly the bank was very spacious, and quite beautiful architecture inside.

For a short time I just stood in the middle of the bank looking back at everyone looking at me. There was no sound or movement at all. I figured if I stood there long enough someone just might come and help me.

Thankfully someone did. He had impeccable English and assisted me greatly and very efficiently as I withdrew local currency from my Diners Card.

I actually felt a little paranoid upon leaving the bank with everyone watching me and knowing I was carrying a sum of cash on me. I hurried back to my room at the hotel as I did not feel safe knowing that people had seen me withdraw cash. I needed to be safe!

I was very aware that I was now on my own and set out hoping I might be able to recognise a funeral parlour or head stone maker. My options were becoming very limited.

I was walking down a shopping area and about twenty yards in front of me an elderly man suddenly raises one arm, points directly at me and starts talking very quickly in a language I was not familiar with. What was so striking about this man, was that as he came closer it was very obvious that he was blind.

Totally blind. All one could see were the whites of his eye balls. There was nothing else, just white eyeballs and he is, as strange as it is to say this, "looking straight at me."

The blind man continued to speak as he walked closer and I was aware that something very special was happening; his message was very important, if only I knew what he was saying. By now I am standing still and he continues to both walk towards me and speak to me. I ask my angels *please help me to remember this and understand what he is saying.*

Suddenly he is standing in front of me, I mean directly in front of me and his arm is still out straight pointing at me as he continues to speak. He actually stopped with his finger pointing at me with about an inch to spare or he would have touched my chest! If it were not for the white eyeballs I would have sworn he could see but the white eyeballs never wavered and he never stopped talking to me.

Suddenly from nowhere he takes the hand that is pointed at me and he lifts the lid off a large, long basket he is carrying.

Strange, I did not see him carrying a basket before perhaps that was because I was so focussed on his white eyeballs and his arm out front with his finger pointing at me. Was he real or was I seeing him with my spiritual eyes? I do not actually know but he certainly seemed real enough.

Still he is talking to me and I am aware how important this moment is – and then it happens.

Oh my God! I wanted the ground to open up and swallow me. A huge snake head rises up from the basket and is looking at me straight in the eyes. I recognise this is a cobra, a very big and dangerous cobra; he is looking at me, his forked tongue is moving in and out of his mouth and the sides of his face start to flare outwards to form his hood.

This is not good I scream within to myself and I learn what it is to feel petrified. I have never been this afraid before in my life. I have never been really, really, afraid before – this was more than being afraid. I was not just afraid I was totally paralytic with fear! Even worse, I found I could not move.

You know, we have all watched movies where the victim stands there like an idiot and you are saying in your mind *Run Run* but the victim doesn't run and just stands there! Well that was me. I just could not move and the snake was well out of the top of the basket now and we were looking eye-level at each other. He is not looking happy at me and I could not move. There would have only been about 6 inches from his head to my face. OMG!

I am aware of my crystal necklace inside my clothing but cannot move to hold it so I beg for help so that I can move.

MOVE! I yell at myself within my mind but I cannot. The snake is moving closer and would be less than one hands length between our eyes. I am petrified! I can see yellow in his colors and I am so close that it is like his skin is made up of bubble type of covering.

I realise I am in deep trouble here and I have to try to find a tactic that will work and help myself to move. The old man has finally stopped talking. What is he waiting for? I do not know. But I know I am in danger and I cannot afford to keep standing still.

So I use all the will in my mind to speak to my toes and tell them to try to move sideways. Inch by inch I slowly begin to move sideways. It is agonising. As I slowly make progress and start to move sideways, the snake moves his head with synchronicity staring at me with his face flared out. I can see the intricate pattern in his face and the colors, I worry about that forked tongue working its way in and out of its mouth.

Things are not looking good!

I can't believe it, I have now moved so far sideways that I can now move forward and still it is painstakingly slow as I inch my way forward. I look directly ahead of me and I do not allow myself to look sideways and see the snake. It takes all my courage not to look at the snake and what he is doing.

I hear the man's voice again, he is retelling the same message as if he wants me to memorize it, but it makes no sense to me. It is strange because all other noises around us has ceased to exist and I do not hear anything but the blind man's voice, but I am not about to look at him or his scary snake!

I have inched my way so far forward that they are now just behind me where we are standing in the street and suddenly I am able to move my foot further than an inch. I am even able to move my foot forward by about a foot's length and I am aware I am leaving the blind man and his snake behind me.

Still the old man recites over and over his message but now I am walking away from him and soon I can start to run.

Oh my, did I run. I just ran and ran and ran until I could no longer run and finally allowed myself to look back behind me, he was gone. There was no blind man with a cobra in sight, I am safe!

I look forward and just then a rickshaw appears and I just climb in, give him the name of my Hotel and I hold myself very stiff watching everyone as we travel the dusty roads just to make sure that there are no more blind men laying in wait for me.

I hold it all together until I reach my room, turn the lock in the door and run to my bed. The tears start to flow and then I am sobbing my heart out, just sobbing and sobbing. It has been such an ordeal.

I have no idea of how much time has passed but right at that moment I did not wish to leave the room. I have this great need to feel safe. What I experienced was more terrifying than having an AK47 shoved in my face with the soldier screaming at me in anger.

I never want to ever see another snake in my life and especially a cobra. It was all just too much for me and I needed to take some time out just for me so that I can come to terms with what just happened.

A COBRA!

CHAPTER TWELVE

AN ANGEL

There was a knock at my door. I hesitated at first to answer – it may have been one of the soldiers. Knock, knock. Only one way to find out, answer the door!

I opened my door carefully and looked out and there stood a very handsome man, he had a white business man's shirt on, black trousers, polished black shoes and he had a huge big smile on his face!

"Hello, I am the Assistant Manager in the Hotel, my name is Ahmid and here is my card."

I took the card and looked at him bewildered.

"I understand you need assistance and I want to help you. May I come in?"

Oh my God, I just wanted to put my arms around him and hug him forever. He had the most impeccable English and I just had this immediate feeling that I was in very safe and efficient hands and it felt like he was an angel sent to help me. He was my angel! *How did he know I needed help?*

Ahmid came in and we talked about why I was here, what I had been trying to achieve and then I showed him my instructions. As he read the paper his face became very serious. Then he explained:

"Because you have spent so much time trying to locate the taxi driver to assist you and now find he is of no help to you, you no longer have the time to go to this place that is described in your instructions. But I have a different place that I would like to take you to and I think you will be very satisfied. First I will take you to the village to meet the family and especially the Uncles that are mentioned. We then need their approval and if all goes well I will hire a van the next day and take you to a very special place. What is your decision?"

Oh gosh what is my decision? I had no idea, but how did he know I needed help? I believed he had been sent to me by my angels and so without taking the time (because we were now running out of time) I had to make a decision on the spot. What will I do?

"Yes! Yes I want to go to this special place you have in mind – I trust you Ahmid and I would be so grateful for your assistance. I have not done well on my own and I really need your help. So yes, my decision is yes."

With that Ahmid gave me another one of his beautiful smiles and told me to be ready at 8.30am in the morning and he would pick me up and we would go to the family.

I cannot begin to explain why I trusted this man on sight and put my life in his hands. It felt like the most natural thing in the world to do and right from the moment I saw him I knew my angels had sent him to me. I had no hesitation to go wherever he wanted to take me.

I was so happy. As I write these words I can see him standing in front of me. He had lovely thick black hair that had a little curl at the end of it. He wore it just above collar length, and he had a wonderful, subtle after shave that seemed to be made especially for him. Ahmid had a little goatie beard that was connected by a straight moustache above his lips and the facial hair went up and met his sideburns. His eyebrows were thick and bushy and his eyes were almost black in color. His lips were full and would be the envy of a lot of the women today who have chemical injections to plump up their lips. This man had it all!

Ahmid was about the same height as I am and he was very fit looking, I would think in tight clothing he would have abs to die for and yet his demeanour was very humble. He seemed completely unaware of the effect he could have on women. And his smile – definitely sent to me by my angels. I really looked forward to the next morning and what we might achieve.

8.30 am I was waiting at the reception area and right on time a van pulls up and Ahmid gets out greeting me and opens the door for me to get in.

As we drove we talked a lot about many different subjects and I learned that this man had university degrees, he was highly qualified but there were few jobs in his field so his chances of improving his employment status were limited. It didn't seem to matter what subject I chose to introduce, he was well versed and I was extremely impressed with his knowledge base.

As we started to leave the city of Jallandhar behind us we passed a very large area of grass which was just full of huge, quite ugly looking very large birds. Just like the bird that had been following me! Up close they were not a pretty looking bird, when I asked Ahmid what they were, I was not surprised to hear they were called the Indian Eagle. Now I knew what had been flying above me so often! Of course it was their eagle, Raema had shown me this type of bird in my visions.

I knew that we had been driving for quite some time but had not kept a close eye on the time, instead I was so interested in the scenery of people, buildings, and even in the middle of nowhere there would be a beautiful Temple which I just had to see. Ahmid was very accommodating. The temple we stopped at was a light aqua color with a gold curved roof and Ahmid said it was real gold. It certainly looked like real gold and inside the Temple was even more gold that were etched in designs around the walls and around supporting poles. There was a glassed warrior, in full regalia, absolutely magnificent with a curved sabre. So I had a history lesson that went back centuries and learned how this particular man, Shr Guru Gobind Singh had fought against 'unruled persons' and always helped the people who needed help. Some of these 'unruled people' he talked about came from the mountains.

My interest was suddenly zooming in on the word 'mountains' because as much as I had looked I had not seen any mountains in the parts of India I had been, yet Raema had most definitely shown me mountains. Big mountains.

We continued on and there was a magnificent field of sunflowers. They were so tall and the flowers blooming were bigger than any I had ever seen before – I just had to ask Ahmid to stop and let me walk amongst them.

I was so amazed, it was easy to walk through the field of sunflowers, they were actually taller than me and my height is five and a half feet tall. The flower blossoms were bigger than my face and I had Ahmid take a photo for me so I could show my family at home just how big these plants grow in the soil in India. This was before the age of digital cameras but he did manage to take a good photo for me.

We seemed to be driving off the main roads and in smaller roads that were leading to other smaller roads and suddenly I felt overwhelmed and said to Ahmid "We are arriving at the village aren't we?"

I had tears streaming down my face with so many mixed emotions but the loudest emotion was *I am coming home, I am coming home.*

Now how could I have possibly known that we were entering the driveway to Raema's family village? There is no way I could have known but every fibre of my being was telling me I had arrived home and the joy I felt was ecstatic.

I never questioned how I knew. I simply knew.

Children ran to greet the vehicle and its occupants and Ahmid spoke in Punjabi to some of them and they ran ahead to announce our arrival.

I was told we were going to the home of Raema's nephew and Ahmid would allow me to enter by myself, he would wait at the van for me.

I seemed to know just where to go and a young man and his wife greeted me and asked me to enter their home and have a drink. They spoke no English but I knew what they meant. They gave me a drink called Lassa and it is absolutely beautiful. I think it has a yoghurt base and is like a glass of milk and somehow they keep it in a big stainless steel container that keeps it cold because it was chilled when they gave it to me. I loved the taste which pleased them immensely.

I had been invited into their home to sit down and their home existed of one square room with a table and two chairs and a small bed against the wall. There was no other furniture but it was welcoming and I was so happy to be there, I had come home!

Then the wife started to wail. Ohhhhh! I will never forget that wail. It is so different to the indigenous Maori people of New Zealand who also wail. Whilst different the Indian wail is totally heart wrenching.

I was taken back to the time I was woken in the funeral home when Raema woke me with her wailing. This was the same. And of course the water works just would not stop. I sobbed and sobbed as I held the containers of Raema on my lap

Suddenly the room was filled with the presence of a man who literally filled the doorway. He had a turban on his head and his clothing was very simple, cotton long shirt with no buttons he would have to pull it over his head and pants similar to what I was wearing, He had both hands on the frame of the doorway and it was as though he filled the room. He was very tall.

I was in awe of his presence and at the same time I knew him. I longed to hold him! I stayed seated not knowing what their protocols were so I waited and it appeared this was the father of the young man whose home I was sitting in.

Then this incredible man took quick and deliberate strides towards me and as quick as lightning he placed his hand upon my head with his fingers holding my head very firmly but not painful at all.

I felt a calmness enter my being and I truly felt as though his hand did more than reach and hold my head; it felt like his hand dipped into my head all the way down to my heart, and his hands cradled my heart. And in this way he "knew" me. He knew everything he needed to know about me and it was a magnificent and very advanced Spiritual Technique to know a person and their worth.

Oh how lonely I felt when he withdrew his hands from my heart. Because that is exactly what it felt like he had done – and in doing so – I knew him!

What an incredible experience. I have never come across the like in my whole life.

It was as though another miracle had come to pass.

Well, I must have passed the test, because this dear elderly gentleman, whose essence filled this home, he knelt at my feet and wept. He wept and wept and wept – and I wept along with him. He was one of the two Uncles I knew I would meet but I had not been prepared for his incredible charisma, and I was so grateful for his humility. In that instance I simply loved this dear man.

There was another surprise yet to come. When I looked into his eyes – they were blue! Have you ever seen an Indian with blue eyes? Well I had not until that moment and they were a very bright clear blue that really stood out.

All the while this was happening, the young wife had been wailing and then she was joined by another woman wailing and she was the wife of Uncle.

When we could compose ourselves Uncle indicated for me to follow him. I thanked the man and wife of the home I had been in and went with Uncle to a smaller home, which apparently was his home and he wanted to show me his treasures, little trinkets that he had hanging on cloth on the wall, And then he had me sit on the only chair in the house and again, knelt at my feet and wept.

Of course my own tears fell as well, the emotion of coming home was so overwhelming and I could feel the love coming from this man in waves as in the sea shore with waves coming in.

So it was with Uncle, his love would continually come in waves to me unconditionally. And bless him, when he saw my tears he took a cloth from his pocket and gently dabbed my tears away and signalled with his finger pointing at my tears and shaking his head no, and I knew he was telling me not to cry but it was alright for him to cry!

CHAPTER THIRTEEN

THE UNCLES

I didn't think I had ever felt as happy as I did with this Uncle with the blue eyes. I felt a beautiful calmness from within. I felt surrounded by love. What more could I ask for. But there was more yet to come!

Uncle took me for a walk, chatting away, knowing I didn't understand a word he said and it didn't matter to either of us. He gently draped one arm across the back of me to my shoulder and it felt like he had tucked me under his arm and he was letting everyone know I was his.

It felt so normal and so right!

We walked a short way along a dirt path and came to another house about the size of the first one I had been to, the one at Uncle's son's house and here was another nephew, the son of another Uncle. He actually spoke a little English but there was something about him that I disliked. He had a bad feeling about him. Awful! I disliked him on sight.

He told me that they had sent someone for his father to come home, he was working in the fields but would be home soon and I was invited in, Uncle stayed outside, no doubt to greet his brother. Suddenly the room was filled with the essence of the second Uncle. No one had told me this Uncle was blind so that was a bit of a shock, I felt so bad for him. But guess what – he also had the brightest, clear blue eyes just like his brother!

However it did not seem to stop him from moving around confidently. He went and sat on the only stool in the house and I just naturally knelt at his feet. Wham! Here we go again, Uncle places his hands and fingers on my head and, like his brother, I feel his fingers go down into my being and gently take hold of my heart. It felt amazing! I *loved* this feeling!

I loved the feeling so much I did not want it to stop, but sadly it did as I felt his hands gently let my heart go and pull out from my body. And I *knew* that he "knew" me.

And then putting both hands gently on either side of my head, this gentle, blind man lovingly holds me – two Uncles with beautiful, bright brilliant blue eyes. I knew I would never see the like again in India.

He wept and wept and wept and the women around us wailed. And I sobbed.

Bless him, when he would feel my tears he would brush them aside for me and then point his finger and shake his head no, but then he would cry again himself.

It was one of the most emotional days I think I have ever spent! And to think of all that time I wasted on the silly taxi man who couldn't speak any English and was of no help to me at all. I thought of all the days I could have been spending with this family but now it was too late.

Ahmid arrived at the door and said it was time for us to leave; he spoke to the Uncles on my behalf and told them we would pick them up very early tomorrow and told them where we were headed. They agreed and were happy about the arrangements. It was very difficult to say goodbye when we had just found one another. Ahmid told me that the first Uncle wanted me to stay the night but Ahmid had to explain we were running out of time and he had to take me back. I was so disappointed I did not have more days as I would have happily stayed with him as primitive as their furnishings were. It did not matter to me, I just wanted to be tucked under his arm.

I kept looking back through the vehicle windows until finally the village was out of sight. I never queried how I knew we were arriving at Raema's village, or why I had felt I came home. It simply was as it was.

CHAPTER FOURTEEN

THE SPECIAL DAY

I arose early and chose an outfit I had not yet worn. It was very beautiful, cobalt blue with beautiful decorations around the neck and I had been saving it for "The Special Day."

And now that Special Day had finally arrived I was very sombre. I wanted to wear my best dress in their local style and I wanted Raema to be proud of me on this day.

For the first time, I wore the necklace on the outside of my clothing and it looked spectacular against the cobalt blue. It truly did.

I was downstairs right on time for Ahmid to collect me and off we drove to the village. We had already discussed Ahmid's desire to leave India and come to New Zealand and I was so comfortable with him I had no hesitation of putting myself forward as his sponsor. He was overjoyed as he said he did not think he could ask me, he did not want me to think he was helping me only to have to repay him for sponsorship to my country so he was full of gratitude that I WANTED to sponsor him. I did not know what it involved but I had a fair idea and I believed that I would be responsible for his wellbeing for at least two years. I was totally on-board with this and I wanted my angel, my brother to be able to come to my homeland. I knew there would be so many opportunities in New Zealand that were not available to him in India and I believed he deserved the chance to prove himself.

So it was a very happy drive for both of us to the village and we were there before we knew it.

However, when Ahmid went to collect the Uncles and bring them to the van, he came back by himself telling me there was a family meeting taking place and some disagreement about where we are taking Raema's ashes.

We entered the home together and I was greeted by both Uncles very lovingly. It appeared that the one causing the problem was the nephew I met yesterday who had a little English and I did not take a liking to him. I disliked him even more when I found out he was the only one protesting about where Raema should go!

"How do we get around this?" I asked Ahmid.

"The only way," he replied "is for you to claim Raema as your mother and you claim the right to make the decision because as her daughter it is your right to make the decision."

Well I was more than ready to take on this nasty nephew so I stood up showing my anger and shouted at him:

"How dare you! How. Dare. You. She is my mother and I am her daughter and you will not interfere, you will have no say because you have none and you are doing nothing but causing interference for the sake of it. So butt out of it buddy because Raema is MY MOTHER!"

Wow I really let go and let him know my anger and you could see him literally cringing away from me as I told it to him as it was, and in the meantime Ahmid is interpreting for the sake of the others and they are all nodding their heads in agreement.

And that's all it took!

It was that easy.

We climbed in the van, the two Uncles of course coming with us but I was not happy to see the nephew that I had taken such a dislike to climbing in with us but it would have been petty of me to insist he get out. He knew where he stood with me and who had won that round so I just let it stand.

As we drove along the road one of the Uncles tapped me on the shoulders and indicated to me that they would like to hold Raema's ashes which were sitting on my knee. I suddenly felt very selfish and knew I should have offered her to them earlier and happily gave Raema into her brothers keeping. Where else would she rather be and I felt her happiness within me of being held within her brother's arms. I watched as tears fell down his cheeks as he quietly talked to his sister giving her his last farewell.

It was a beautiful moment even in its sadness. I could see she was deeply loved. I was so happy for her. That sounds a silly thing to say, but she was home in her brothers arms where she wanted to be.

Then something extraordinary had happened. I had not noticed it at first, so busy talking and turning and talking to the Uncles and talking with Ahmid – I became aware that we were starting to drive uphill rather than the usual flat roads we had been driving on.

Hills! Mountains! Oh my God, Raema had taken me to mountains and this is her Special Day and here we are going uphill so steeply I cannot see over the top of the rise.

I am in awe!

CHAPTER FIFTEEN

DIMENSIONAL SOUND SHIFTS

I started looking around, taking in the landscape. We had been driving for about six to seven hours by now and there were hills around me and mountains behind them and I am thinking to myself *when did this happen?*

After all this time I finally see something other than the flat land that had surrounded me. We are climbing and still climbing and I can hear the engine in the van straining at times.

The van is very simple, it has a door and seats and that's it, no mats on the floor just the bare metal floor and at times holes in the floor so that you can see the road rushing by underneath you.

Ahmid said we would be stopping soon, he knew a spot a little further along where it was flat and safe to pull off the road and he needed to take a small break and it would give us all a break from the long journey.

I thought *gosh I wonder how much further we have to go poor Ahmid has to do all the driving!*

We hit the top of a rise we are driving along and in the distance I can see a beautiful mountain, it is exquisite and I ask Ahmid does he know what it is called?

"That is Nanda Devi Mountain," Ahmid tells me. When I arrive back in New Zealand I look it up on the map and it is the second highest mountain in India! Oh wow, I had never expected Raema would bring me to the Himalayans! It is part of the Garwhal Himalayans and is located in the state of Uttarakhand. Its name means *Bliss Giving Goddess* and has a religious significance.

I look closely and I can see a Temple on the top of the mountain, and I can actually see the flat roof and people moving around. I ask Ahmid what that Temple is called and he looked at me hard and long and then he tells me that that the Temple is called Nainda Devis which means Top of the Hill. He tells me that only very spiritual people are allowed to go there, and only very spiritual people are allowed to see it.

When I arrived home in New Zealand and saw the photos I sobbed my heart out, my common sense told me that there was no way I could see a temple that high up, and yet it was as clear as daylight to me.

Miracles keep unfolding!

And I know Raema knows where she is!

It wasn't long and we pulled into what would equate to a petrol station and Ahmid came back with extra bottles of water for everyone and sandwiches which was most considerate of him.

Raine

Then we travelled probably a few more miles and pulled over at a very good stopping place. It was flat and off the road enough to be safe but truthfully there was very little traffic on the road. I had absolutely no idea where we were but we were a long way from my Hotel!

I was so excited – mountains, finally I am starting to see mountains. Not only mountains but the Himalayan Mountains!

We all quickly ate and drank and stretched and then it was time to get back into the van. I was about to step forward when something extraordinary happened to me.

Try to imagine what I am going to describe to you.

There was a mega sound of thunderclap, fine-tuned to the sharpness you'd expect from a recoiling whip, crackling through the air – right in front of you – filling up all the spaces to your left as well as to your right!

If I were to simplify it I would say SNAP, CRACKLE, POP.

SNAP – wakeup call

CRACKLE – break through dimensional sound barriers

POP – alter molecular formations out of third dimensional limitations.

My necklace, it was as though upon the Dimensional Sound Shift the necklace was literally thrown away from me and hit the dirt a good two yards away from me!

Who broke it and threw it away? I do not know. In my mind I remembered Jimmy saying to me *there are bad energies trying to stop you, you need protection!*

I was in shock. Ahmid had seen it happen he also was shocked and then he rushed forward and said "Do not worry Sister I will collect all the pieces and restring them for you."

Well we searched and we searched. It was just a plain red dirt area we were in, nowhere for beads to hide even small ones, but we could not find all the pieces. I was devastated. I had never had anything like this happen to me before.

And sure enough, true to his word, Ahmid restrung the necklace together again and then put it over my neck. But it was nowhere as long as it was before; there were many pieces we were unable to find. How was that possible? We were sitting inside the van at this stage.

SNAP.
CRACKLE.
POP.

The Dimensional Sound Shifts surrounds me and breaks the necklace and throws the necklace away from me. We hear the beads as they all hit the floor of the van. I look at Ahmid in shock and he looks back at me with his mouth wide open.

"It will be alright, please do not be upset Sister I will fix this for you. We are in the van we will find all the pieces," Ahmid says to me.

We search every inch if the van, after all it is not very hard to do so there is no carpet just the metal floor. Ahmid even gets out of the van, walking around it and checking underneath the van. Then he restrings the necklace. But more pieces are missing!

Ahmid holds the necklace up after he has restrung it. It is about a third of the size it originally was.

What am I going to tell Jimmy? I sob inside myself. I can't believe this is happening on this most special of Special Days.

I look at the necklace and I say to Ahmid, "Thank you Ahmid but I think this time I will not wear it, besides I do not think there is enough left to go over my head, I will put it safely in my bag."

I am very quiet for a while as we drive along the road, continually climbing. I keep thinking about the thunderous Dimensional Sound Shift that keeps happening around me. What is out there that is so strong to cause such a reaction and what is the gift of the crystals to act as payment to protect me? Because crystals were disappearing at an alarming rate!

What is it or rather who is it that wants to harm me so much?

It is a disconcertaining feeling to say the least.

A monkey suddenly runs across the road in front of our van and gets my attention. I look around and I see a forest, and as I look higher still I see a large cavern and I hear Raema's voice saying to me *and this is the jewel I am saving for you.*

I ask Ahmid where we are and he tells me, "This is the Link Road of Anand Pur Sahib and this is a very special forest, it is a forest for the spirits because at night time the spirits walk these forests."

I smile to myself recognising the forest that Raema had shown me in her visions. She knew all along she was going to come to this place – she just needed to orchestrate it into a reality!

Smart lady!

I know we are on the right road and still we continue to climb.

I think of this phenomenon that has happened to me. I am going to suggest that sound barriers exist outside our third dimensional reality and extend into other dimensional existences. I consider that "Dimensional Shifting through Sound" can bring about altered molecular structure as we recognise structure in this existence, and I further suggest that we are able to bring about this Sound Shifting without mechanical intervention.

I believe that has been proven by the total disappearance of most of the large and some of the small beads of beautiful crystals, moonstone, amethyst, etc. that made up my crystal necklace. There are theories that crystals make their own sound and I believe these sounds have been actually recorded by a scientist in the United Kingdom. He has actually sold CD's of crystals making sounds.

Did the high frequency sound from the crystals access a dimensional shift and not actually disappear at all simply molecularly removed themselves from our third dimension?

Is this a New Age theory? Hardly, history is full of amazing feats connected with the vibration of sound.

Just to bring one example to mind – we're all no doubt familiar with the defeat of Jericho – "the walls came tumbling down." How was this achieved? Well the stories would have us believe that something as simple as sound could bring about destruction and annihilation. But it's just a story . . . . right?

Certainly gives you something to think about doesn't it. Well I don't have to think about it, I lived it!

And miracles continued around me!

CHAPTER SIXTEEN

OUR SPECIAL DAY CONTINUES

E ven with all that has happened, I continue to feel very confident that the day will end the way it should. I look forward to the next landmark that Raema showed me through her visions.

We continue on our long drive and then I realise we are slightly going downhill.

We emerge from the forestry area and there in front of me is another miracle!

I see the mountain cut into a U shape and a village built inside it! I can actually see it with mine own eyes, and yet I had clearly seen it with my spiritual eyes when Raema had shown me this landmark when I was in New Zealand and she was in a coma in hospital!

There is no question to me that we are going to the place Raema had wanted to go to all along and I think how amazingly beautiful that is!

"We are not far now are we, this is the last village?" I said to Ahmid.

He looked at me with shock knowing I had not travelled this road before and said "Yes my Sister, this is the last village. You have been given very special eyes with which to see." It was a lovely compliment coming from Ahmid.

It wasn't much further and we turned off the road and down a fairly well used road and arrived at a very beautiful temple. There, across from us, is where they say the mouth of the Ganges River starts. Across the river is a huge mountain that reaches very high into the air. I am so grateful to have Ahmid with me. I want to explain to the Uncles that I have not seen Raema for a long time and why. But as I try to explain they did not have the need to know, after all, they "knew" me and that was enough.

"Let us get on with the formalities," said one of the Uncles.

I would have had no idea what to do. Ahmid truly was my angel.

We had to line up at a separate building from the Temple and once inside, we paid a fee and we registered Raema's details into their log book. So everything that is done there has a record, isn't that wonderful to know!

Once we had our records completed we were allowed to enter the Temple, the Uncles each carried their sister's ashes. There was a large notice board with a message on it and I asked Ahmid what it said.

"Every day they take a saying from the Book of Records and they post it for everyone to see. Today's saying is: Today is the right day."

Wow, how appropriate was that!

I followed and copied whatever Ahmid and the Uncles did so I did not embarrass them and eventually we made our way out to the river.

The Uncle who could see took his blind brother's hand and Ahmid guided me knee deep into the water. By now I was holding both containers of ashes and slowly I removed the lid of one, and then the lid of the other and I passed one of the containers to Uncle who could see and I kept one and we slowly let Raema's ashes go into the river. The tears just flowed down my cheeks, it was such a spiritual moment, and then to top it all off, oh how could I ever have asked for more – there was a huge eagle who came flying from around the corner of the mountain cawing. Cawing just as in my visions. It was heart wrenching, it was beyond any experience I had ever known before. It was so beautiful, it was so sad. There were so many contradictions in my feelings, but most of all, I knew I was blessed.

And miracles continued around me!

I washed out my container so Uncle did the same and putting the lid on the now empty containers, both Uncles now had a container each. I took out the bright, mustard cover made from crushed velvet and gave it to the Uncles also. It had served well and now it would be well loved by these two brothers whom I knew would share it. It would be particularly comforting for the blind Uncle as he would appreciate its lovely feel.

Both Uncles now stripped down to their underwear and went into the Ganges River washing themselves and Ahmid followed suit so I walked away giving them some privacy for what was obviously a religious ceremony to them. I presumed the nephew I did not like was there as well, I just needed some time to myself.

I sat under a beautiful tree and Ahmid came rushing up to me all excited. "Come, come you must see it is very auspicious there are two cobra's and they are having a fight, such timing is amazing." He was so excited.

I was not quite as ecstatic as Ahmid was and trailed slowly behind him. Apparently because the cobras were fighting immediately after releasing Raema's ashes it was seen as good luck! Mmmm. I have to pass on that one, my experiences up close to a cobra had not been what I would call 'good luck.' However I do understand that the cobra is revered in India so some would say my experience was one of good luck. Unfortunately I cannot see it quite that way!

There was some food handed to each of us, it was similar to rice with cumin held inside thin patties of Roti which is a pancake type of bread the Indian people make. It is delicious, it was then time to be back in the van as we made our way to a second Temple.

This second Temple was beyond anything I had ever seen to date. It was just incredibly beautiful!

There were large white domes on top of the temple and the domes were etched with gold on the top. The size of the premises was massive. I was totally gobsmacked with the beauty of this temple. We all had to remove our shoes and it was very hot on my feet. I was probably the only one not used walking barefoot and now I am walking on huge marble tiles exposed to the sun so you can imagine how hot they are in this heat wave. There are queues in front of us, we were not moving fast, I probably looked ridiculous hopping from one foot to the other. Finally we reached some shade and could enter the temple.

As beautiful as this Temple was on the outside, the inside was majestic! I had never seen anything in my life that was so aesthetically decorated.

After we had attended to the formalities at this Temple we were led outside to an area where people were sitting against the wall and we joined them, quickly being served with the very best Dahl I have ever eaten! The water that was served was direct from the Himalayas and it was so delicious. I am not a person who enjoys drinking water but oh my, I could drink this water all day every day it was so fresh and beautiful to drink, no chemicals just pure spring water. I was most grateful for it in the heat we were experiencing.

It was quite stunning looking out from the veranda to the Himalaya mountains. I felt so many blessings this day!

CHAPTER SEVENTEEN

THE LAST FAREWELL

We all climbed into the van again, it was getting quite late now but there was still some light. We were close to a main road when we had a break-down, one of the back wheels was flat and the wheel needed changing.

I was happy to spend this time with the Uncles as I had been told they would take the train back to their village and we would continue back to the Hotel on our own.

The Uncles just broke their hearts and sobbed and sobbed as we said goodbye and of course I was in no better state. It was the saddest thing I was asked to do, to say our goodbyes. How could I say goodbye to these beautiful people who had shown me so much love and care and honoured me. As the wheel was just put back together, the Uncles and nephew had to walk away. I watched them with a broken heart and in the end had to get into the van and cry my heart out.

Suddenly I felt something happening within me.

What's going on? I thought to myself. And then I *knew!*

I was aware of a movement within my chest and slowly it took shape, sort of cylinder if I were to try to name a shape, and it gently moved up my neck up through my skull, and I actually felt movement lift off my shoulders as the internal movement left through the top of my head!

Raema was leaving me! I understood so many things in that moment. I understood that the Uncles knew their sister's spirit had taken up residence inside my being and they recognized her, hence it broke their heart to walk away and leave me, and thus finally leave their sister. It did not change their love for me, in fact in intensified it.

I understood why I knew I was *home* when we arrived at her village for the first time and I think I knew then that she was working with me but I had not recognised to what extent she was working within me.

I actually felt Raema's spirit leave my body! No wonder her ashes were so light to carry around, I had her to help me carry them.

It is a most blessed experience I think I will ever have, to be aware of a loving spirit taking their leave out of my top chakra.

I felt her spirit leave me!

I sat there feeling so many feelings all at once, shock, love, thankfulness, gratefulness but most of all I thanked Raema for bringing me safely to India to bring her home. I loved her, I loved her so much in that moment she really and truly was my mother.

I don't think I can ever find the words to describe just how loved I felt.

And miracles abound around me.

You cannot know how hard it was to say goodbye that last time to Raema. It is almost too sacred to try to tell you.

CHAPTER EIGHTEEN

FAREWELL TO MY ANGEL

I had so much to be thankful to Ahmid for. I wrote him a letter the night before it was time for me to leave telling him how much his being there had meant to me. I knew he would not accept any money from me so I slipped some inside my letter and sealed the envelope.

It was with such sadness that we arrived at the railway station and I was with him as he purchased my railway ticket. A whole 200 Rupees!

I knew immediately Ahmid purchased the railway ticket that I had been ripped off big time in New Delhi and I pieced together what I believe happened. I am quite sure that the man who I gave my passport to, so he could purchase my railway ticket – well I believe they had set me up from the beginning. With my passport he could probably find out just how much cash I was carrying, and then they had the baggage carrier ready and waiting for me and it was no doubt that baggage carrier who stole my wallet.

They must have been pretty angry that there was very little money in my wallet hence it was thrown away and the police man knew where to bring it. Was the policeman in it too? I will never know but I have my thoughts. Wow what a string of events extending from a greedy rickshaw driver!

Now it was time to say goodbye to Ahmid. He had brought me on-board the train and given me my instructions, "Do not talk to anyone," he said to me. And he cried. Oh how he cried, and yes I bawled my eyes out it was so sad a moment and I felt we had shared so much in such a short space of time.

I went to put my envelope in his upper pocket and he moved away shaking his head NO but I said to him I have written him a letter and he had to read it so eventually he agreed to accept it. I had told him in my letter to consider the cash I had left with him to go towards his plane fare for when he joins me in New Zealand, he was my brother and I loved him unconditionally and there was no question of sponsoring him to New Zealand. I wanted him to come!

I cried my eyes out as the train pulled out, putting my head out the window until I could no longer see him and then I sat in my seat and cried and cried for him. I missed him so badly.

I wrote to him from New Delhi. I wrote to him when I arrived home in New Zealand. And then I received a letter that would tear my heart in two.

This letter was written by Ahmid's father who was an engineer on a ship, and he writes: "I am informing you with a heavy heart full of grief that my one child (son) Ahmid, expired in the Hotel in Jallandhar. After completing his nightshift he went to his hotel room and next morning they found him dead.

I received this news at sea and now got down from the ship at first port of ship call. My son's body has already been cremated. I shall be taking his ashes to Kerat Pur Sahib. I am proceeding home by earliest possible means as my wife is all alone."

My beautiful angel was gone, how could this be. Ahmid was only 27 years old! He passed away in his sleep and he must have talked so much to his parents about me that his father took the time to send a quick letter to me before he had even managed to get home to his wife.

I felt so honoured, so sad, so heartbroken for his parents. No one now to look after them in their old age. How could this be?

It gave me some comfort that I knew where they were taking his ashes, the same place we had taken Raema's ashes and it was a place I knew that he loved.

I am never without my beautiful angel in my heart and my prayers and am so grateful he was there for me before he was called home.

He really was my angel!

THE CRYSTAL NECKLACE

I had arrived back in New Delhi and had my driver take to me another hotel. I did not want to see the rickshaw driver I had last time. I wanted a room with a key in it so having chosen the name of another hotel I asked the driver to take me there.

I don't remember the name of the hotel but thank goodness I asked my driver to wait for me; because I asked to see the room, I wanted to check there was a key you see. I was not prepared for the huge gaping big hole in the wall in the room that was absolutely filthy and ran back to the taxi saying "get me out of here please, now!"

The foolish man from the hotel was calling after me "please madam, I can show you a better room." *Well why didn't you show it to me in the first place!!!!*

I checked only one more hotel and was very satisfied, and then I had to face my phone call to Jimmy and ask if we can meet tomorrow. Somehow I had to put him off asking me about the crystal necklace until I could see him and tell him face to face.

So I telephoned Jimmy. And what are his first words to me? "How is the necklace?"

Oh my God I did not want to tell him on the phone so I pretended I had not heard him and asked if we could meet tomorrow. But no, Jimmy wouldn't have any of it, he kept asking until I finally said to him "Oh Jimmy I have to talk to you about the necklace, something kept breaking it and now more than half is missing!"

"Oh darling don't you worry," Jimmy said with kindness. "Don't you know? That's why I gave it to you."

Ahhhhh! I wanted to scream! Why had he not told me about this before? I had been fretting my heart out about this necklace.

So the next day we met and he looked at the pitiful amount of crystals that were left and I felt so uncomfortable, but Jimmy with his goodness of heart said to me "Never mind, I will restring it myself."

Jimmy shut his shop early that night and he went home, he sat by candle light and he restrung a beautiful crystal necklace.

"What do you think happened to it?" he asked me as we met the day after. "I held it up and the spirits threw it away from me and broke it! And pieces were missing!" Straining his eyes by candlelight Jimmy restrung another necklace for me – and the same thing happened to him as had happened to me in Punjab. So he said to no one in particular - "Alright I will give her something else!"

Which found us back at his jewellery shop where he chose something else for me to take home, but not as amazing as that crystal necklace was but who was I to complain.

I knew the time had now come for me to make a decent purchase to thank Jimmy for all he had done for me and given up. I chose an exquisite ruby marquisate silver bracelet, it is one of my prized possessions and I love it. It carries so many memories! I also had it valued when I arrived home and it came to the exact value I had paid Jimmy. He did well by me, he did not take advantage of me in any way and he was left out of pocket because of the crystal necklace.

I am so grateful to Jimmy for being with me at that very moment the spirits spoke to him and assisted me. He was their instrument and I was travelling blind.

So many miracles opened the way for me. I have so much to give gratitude for.

CHAPTER TWENTY

LAST DAY BEFORE LEAVING INDIA

I had this one single day that was mine, all mine and I decided I wanted to go to the Taj Mahal. Having made arrangements through the hotel I was staying in, my day began with an early pick up.

It was going to be a long day. We were told there would be plenty of stops along the way. We stopped at a place called Midway Hotel Restaurant for lunch and refreshments and it was so lovely to see both an elephant and camel come into the front of the hotel. Obviously the purpose was to try to strum up some business from those of us on the bus however we were all tired and just as happy to admire the animals from afar.

We stopped at the mega Agra Fort in Agra. It was immense for want of a more descriptive word and so, so beautiful. It had been the home of Shah Jahen and his wife Mumtaz Mahal. It was Shah Jahen who had built the Taj Mahal for his wife.

Mumtaz Mahal died giving birth to her fourteenth child. Of these fourteen children, only six lived. One of the sons that survived actually imprisoned his father I think for about twenty odd years and he murdered the rest of his brothers. Such a loving family!

After we enter Fort Agra there is a very steep incline to enter the Fort proper and the buildings are of such an immense size. Immediately we could hear the buzzing of bees.

At one time the British soldiers took up residence in these opulent settings!

We were very fortunate to have such a good guide with excellent English. It is inside the Agra Fort that the Persian Throne once sat! The chair was now in some museum basement in Arabia which seemed such a waste of something so beautiful and historic. The diamond from the throne is actually in Queen Elizabeth's Crown!

Looking over the wall at Agra Fort the moat is dry with red soil, but in the winter the water rises and forms a double moat surrounding the Fort.

We travel past the town where Krishna was born and travel on to the Taj Mahal. On arrival the gates are massive; they have such a presence and are the largest gates I have ever seen.

Upon entering the gates there is still a long walk to be able to enter through another gate which leads to the Taj Mahal complex. On the long pathway to this gate there are magnificent buildings that line both sides of the path and this again is where the British took up residence for their soldiers.

Approaching the gateway again we hear the bees humming as we did at Agra Fort. The gateway is inlaid with precious jewels, scriptures and the Holy Koran. Quite some feat if you could see the size of it!

From inside the gateway looking up, you can read the 41st scripture from the Holy Koran.

There is nothing to prepare you for how beautiful the Taj Mahal is. It is absolutely exquisite, there is a long waterway leading up to it and it already looks gigantic and yet as you come closer it is bigger still. The Taj was built in 1468AD.

I had made friends with a fellow passenger who worked for the United Nations and we took photos for one another on our respective cameras. We happened to be travelling on the same flight to Thailand so once our flight arrived we shared a taxi into the city.

It took 32,000 Artesians, working night and day for two years to complete the Taj Mahal. Pretty impressive. It is made from marble and is one if the seventh wonders of the world.

The Taj Mahal is perfect in its geometry and symmetry. The Taj Mahal is surrounded by four towers two on either side. They are slightly leaning outwards so that if there was ever a calamity that caused them to fall, then they would fall outwards and not damage the Taj Mahal.

Precious stones are inlaid into the marble of the Taj Mahal that include moonstone, carnelian, malachite, agate, gold, silver, etc.

There are three gates ahead of us, the first one we enter takes us into the Taj Mahal. The second to a huge building that acts as a guest house and the building on the other side of the Taj Mahal faces Mecca and acts as a Mosque.

Looking down the river from the Taj Mahal we can see the Agra Fort where the Shah was imprisoned for twenty odd years by his son. It had to feel like such a long time before he could join his beloved wife.

I thought it was lovely that we were able to go downstairs to view the incredibly beautiful inlaid coffins of the Shah and his wife. I have never seen coffins so decorative and could not imagine how many men it would take to lift the lid let alone the whole coffin! I believe now they have roped this area off and people cannot go there anymore because of the fear of disintegration but from what I saw they were going to be around for a few more centuries.

We stopped at incredible Forts in Akbar before returning to New Delhi and just as we arrived back there was a beautiful sunset settling over New Delhi. It had been a long day but my only day. So I say I have had a journey to India and I had a trip. Today was my trip. My sightseeing day!

The next day I had a very long flight to Bangkok flying Thai Airways who were absolutely beautiful to fly with.

They say flying is not without its problems and a truer word is never said. We were all asked at the airport in India to identify our luggage before they boarded it on the plane. I was amongst just two others that they seemed to have "lost' our suitcases and of course they had to be found before we could fly!

Farewell India. So much for me to process, I need time to take it all in but I am happy flying out even though my "Delhi Belly" has started up again and I am not feeling very well.

I was very fortunate in that the plane was not very full so I could choose where to sit and I could lay down over three seats and try to rest, but that was too much to hope for when I spent most of the time in the airplanes toilets!

Not much rest!

CHAPTER TWENTY ONE

GURU IN BANGKOK

I arrived somewhat exhausted in Bangkok, having just an overnight stay in New Delhi then off on the big budgie again wending my way home.

I stayed at Kao Sarn Privacy Guesthouse which unfortunately did not have a lift and I had to hike my luggage up several floors in a weakened state.

My room was clean and the bathroom was clean so I was happy. It was the middle of the day and Bangkok was buzzing so I took myself for a little walk, being careful not to get lost as I was aware how tired my body was. I kept an eye out for any food I might be able to tolerate but mostly I just wanted drinks and that was what I stayed with. I just had this one afternoon and the morning then I would fly out just after noon.

Whilst I was out walking I desperately needed to use a bathroom and found a public toilet that had a lady sitting outside and you had to pay her to enter the facilities and she gave you a small amount of toilet tissue to use. I have a horror or spiders and cannot bear to be near cockroaches. Well the facilities were made up of a hole in the floor and whilst I was otherwise occupied a HUGE cockroach walked into the facilities and there was not a lot of room between the walls for me to move away from him. It was a terrifying moment for me as I was unable to just up and rush out, my need was so great and I had to watch this very frightening cockroach as I cleaned up and could finally leave. I decided I would not use another such facility I would just have to wait until I could get back to my Guesthouse!

The time actually went quickly and I guess a lot of that can be contributed to my fatigue and not feeling too well and not looking forward to yet another long journey home.

I spent a restless night up and down to the bathroom and hoped I could get some rest on my way home on the plane the next day. I had been so comfortable in my clothing from Punjab that I just kept wearing them, they were just so comfy.

I rose early the next day and anyone who has been to Bangkok knows the city never sleeps, the streets are constantly busy and there are people elbow to elbow trying to make their way to wherever they are heading.

But I found a different Bangkok.

I stepped out onto the street and it was all but barren. There was not one vehicle on the street I was on and there seemed to be no people rushing around. No noise.

I looked up toward the end of my street and in the middle of the road there stands this fairly big fat Indian man with a smile on his face.

Oh well I have had so many extraordinary things happen to me what's another one?

By now it was almost commonplace for me to have extraordinary things happen around me!

So I walk towards this man, and his smile gets bigger. I continue to slowly walk towards him, and still his smile grows even bigger.

I stop a few yards short of him and he says to me "I am an Indian Guru Master and I have been waiting for you. Shall we sit down?"

And low and behold if there isn't two chairs and a small table.

Still there is no traffic no people rushing by and since when are there table and chairs on the side of the street? But oh well, this is what I have learned to expect. I sit down.

Again he repeats to me that he is an Indian Guru Master and that he has been waiting for me, and with my permission, he takes my hand in his and he reads my life up until this present time. He has not been wrong, he has been spot on, and he hasn't missed a beat. WOW!

He then writes on a piece of paper and scrunches it up so I cannot see what he has written on it.

"Please, blow on it three times for me," he asks.

And I blow three times.

The Indian Guru Master then tells me that he has written a letter, a number and then two more letters. He tells me the first letter is the first letter of my mother's name.

I have a look, wow, he got it right, and it is indeed the first letter of my mother's name!

He then tells me he has written a number and that number represents the number of children I have.

He waits for me to look – oh my God he has it right again. *How is he doing this?*

Then he tells me the other letters he wrote are the beginning letters of my children's names – and again he has it right.

I am blown away!

And then he asks for my hand again, and this time he tells me what the future holds for me – both the good and the bad. At that time I would not have held much faith in what he had said to me, but so far he has not missed a beat, he has been spot on, so I pretty much believe I know what is still to come in my life. I await what the Universe holds in store for me.

He then told me that I had been sent on a sacred mission, and I have completed what I was sent for – now it was to go home.

We stood up and I thanked him and he bowed to me and repeated, "I have been waiting for you." And then he was not there, he was gone, where did he go?

I looked around me and there were no two chairs and a table, the cars were beeping trying to make their way up the street and there were people elbow to elbow walking the streets.

Had I stepped into another dimension? Is there any other possible answer? I feel like a stunned mullet as the saying goes.

Slowly I make my way back to my hotel and collect my things ready to make my way to the airport.

Did that just happen?

CHAPTER TWENTY TWO

HOME SWEET HOME

I had another difficult flight home to New Zealand. The airline facilities and I were good friends, so much so that I was last off the plane struggling to cope with the horrific diarrhoea that I was suffering from. At least now that I was home I could get some medication that I could trust and build my strength up again.

I knew that I had lost a lot of weight and I had only been away for three weeks but it felt like a lifetime with all the things I had gone through.

I came through Customs and collected my luggage, had it x-rayed then moved out looking forward to meeting my family. Except there was no one waiting for me!

Oh they have been held up, I shall go and sit down and wait I thought to myself – and so finding what I thought was an obvious seat with my suitcase and black bag I waited. I waited. I waited. An hour went by and I began to worry so I thought maybe they have missed me and are sitting somewhere else!

So I got up and began to walk around, I knew better than to leave my suitcase behind. There are continual broadcasts that no suitcases are to be left unattended. So I carry my bags and I walk around the airport – it is not such a big area but it sure feels like it at the moment, only because I am so tired. I know I am not thinking as clearly as I should either, so I must be fairly dehydrated by now.

I see a little girl and she looks familiar so I go closer, but I am not sure, *is that my little girl?* I have to go closer still and before I know it I am standing right in front of them.

"Mummy, my mummy!!!" she happily calls out and rushes to hug me. *Yes it is my daughter.*

"Where have you been I have been waiting over an hour?"I asked. But they had not seen me. Or more truthfully, they had not recognised me. I had lost so much weight, and then they were not looking for someone dressed in Indian clothing so they overlooked me and were still waiting for me to come out!

I was happy to be home and on medication, beginning to feel more like myself and making sure to get plenty of fluids into myself.

I had quite a report to make to Raema's son but where did I begin. I had been taking lots of photos as I went along. Whilst in Bangkok I took the time to have them developed so they helped me enormously to lay my story out.

Tears fell down my cheeks freely as I would tell each part of my journey as I knew how important it was to tell it all. I truly broke my heart when I tried to find the Temple on top of Nanda Devi Mountain in the Himalayas and realised it was with my spiritual eyes and not my mortal eyes that I had been privileged to see this special portal in time. I remembered how Ahmid had looked at me at that moment and held my eye for a long time before he answered.

When he had farewelled me at the railway station he told me he knew I was a very special person and that he knew he would never meet anyone like me again in his lifetime. I understood more why he had said that when I looked at this beautiful mountain – Nanda Devi and knew that the Temple on the top of the hill were only shown to a few.

I felt so humble from my journeys and was so overwhelmed by my many possessions in my house when the Uncles had nothing. It made me feel unclean and it took a long time for me to come to terms with accepting this was my life in New Zealand.

When Ahmid's fathers letter came it was a huge blow to me, and I felt that he had finished his lessons on this earth, was kept here a little longer to help me and now that I was safe, he could go home. My angel was gone.

I will forever be full of gratitude to Raema for the learnings she opened me up to and every year I honour her anniversary.

Miracles happen every day!

How many of us simply "do not see"?

I am grateful for the many miracles that I did experience and see. These will always be with me.

CHAPTER TWENTY THREE

RAINE'S THANKS

I wish to thank all those that made the publication of this book possible. Most especially I thank Raema, an old woman whom I came to love so much. She truly became my mother. She took me on miraculous journeys that have empowered me and given me a greater understanding of spirit.

Thank you Jia Sen for the most beautiful book cover. This is the third book Jia and I have worked together on. She is truly amazing and very intuitive. I have Jia to thank for catching your eye when you looked at my book!

Thank you again to Balboa Press; I am most grateful that you have published this book and opened up new arenas for me. In addition Balboa Press has republished my first two award winning books which I hope you will all enjoy. Thank you Balboa Press for looking after me so very well. I am very blessed!

To those special people whom I love, thank you for previewing the book for me and providing me with reviews to help readers understand how the book affected you. You are greatly valued and I could not end this book without including you with thankfulness. You each know who you are, my work would not be complete without you. I love each one of you and you each help me to aspire to higher and higher things with my writing.

My thanks to the organizers of The Author Show for awarding me 1st Prize in "50 Great Writers That You Should Be Reading." Such a prestigious award.

"May your Higher Self always teach you with Grace, and may you always learn in Peace . . ."

Raine

Printed in the United States
By Bookmasters